T0329136

Cambridge Elements

Elements in Applied Social Psychology
edited by
Susan Clayton
College of Wooster, Ohio

THE PSYCHOLOGY OF EFFECTIVE ACTIVISM

Robyn Gulliver
The University of Queensland

Susilo Wibisono
The University of Queensland

Kelly S. Fielding
The University of Queensland

Winnifred R. Louis
The University of Queensland

CAMBRIDGE
UNIVERSITY PRESS

CAMBRIDGE
UNIVERSITY PRESS

University Printing House, Cambridge CB2 8BS, United Kingdom

One Liberty Plaza, 20th Floor, New York, NY 10006, USA

477 Williamstown Road, Port Melbourne, VIC 3207, Australia

314–321, 3rd Floor, Plot 3, Splendor Forum, Jasola District Centre,
New Delhi – 110025, India

103 Penang Road, #05–06/07, Visioncrest Commercial, Singapore 238467

Cambridge University Press is part of the University of Cambridge.

It furthers the University's mission by disseminating knowledge in the pursuit of
education, learning, and research at the highest international levels of excellence.

www.cambridge.org
Information on this title: www.cambridge.org/9781108972109
DOI: 10.1017/9781108975476

First published 2021

A catalogue record for this publication is available from the British Library.

ISBN 978-1-108-97210-9 Paperback
ISSN 2631-777X (online)
ISSN 2631-7761 (print)

The Psychology of Effective Activism

Elements in Applied Social Psychology

DOI: 10.1017/9781108975476
First published online: July 2021

Robyn Gulliver
The University of Queensland

Susilo Wibisono
The University of Queensland

Kelly S. Fielding
The University of Queensland

Winnifred R. Louis
The University of Queensland

Author for correspondence: Winnifred Louis, w.louis@psy.uq.edu.au

Abstract: This Element reviews the social psychology of effective collective action, highlighting the importance of considering activists' goals, time frames, and psychological perspectives in seeking to conceptualise this construct. A novel framework, 'ABIASCA', maps effectiveness in relation to activists' goals for mobilisation and change (Awareness raising; Building sympathy; turning sympathy into Intentions; turning intentions into Actions; Sustaining groups over time; Coalition-building; and Avoiding opponents' counter-mobilisation). We also review the DIME model of Disidentification, Innovation, Moralisation, and Energisation, which examines the effects of failure in creating trajectories of activists' disidentification from collective action; innovation (including to radicalisation or deradicalisation); and increased moral conviction and energy. The social psychological drivers of effective collective action for four audiences are examined in detail, in four sections: for the self and supporters, for bystanders, for opponents, and for third parties. We conclude by highlighting an agenda for future research and drawing out key messages for scholars.

Keywords: collective action, social movements, protest, dissent, political engagement

ISBNs: 9781108972109 (PB), 9781108975476 (OC)
ISSNs: 2631-777X (online), 2631-7761 (print)

Contents

1 Introduction

Collective action can change the world. It is the basis of social movements and, at its best, transforms society by providing the means through which individuals can express dissent and demand a better future. It can take place offline on the streets, online via social media platforms, in a politician's office, or in homes in quiet suburban blocks. It can involve violent or non-violent force. Whatever form it takes, those who engage in collective action share one aspiration: to play a part in generating, celebrating or resisting social change.

At first it may seem obvious what effective collective action would look like. The labour and union movements have a proud history of demanding and winning economic gains for workers, for example (Bradley, 2011). Women around the world have engaged in hunger strikes, demonstrations, and community canvassing to secure the same rights as their male counterparts, with a century of achievements accrued in response (Gouws & Coetzee, 2019). In more recent decades, new movements have won LGBTIQA+ and disability rights, or elevated demands for the rights of nature (e.g., Della Porta & Rucht, 1995; Louis et al., 2020). When looking back on the arc of social movements over the centuries it is tempting to consider these movements as irresistible, unstoppable forces, united in their demands and united in action.

Yet this surface analysis ignores the complex dynamics of social movements, which are composed of a multitude of actions undertaken by a multitude of actors, operating within disparate groups and factions, all with potentially different motivations and goals (Louis & Montiel, 2018; Smith, Livingstone, & Thomas, 2019; Sweetman, Leach, Spears, Pratto, & Saab, 2013; Uluğ & Acar, 2018; van Zomeren & Louis, 2017). Thus, to understand the effectiveness of collective action it is also necessary to understand the psychological processes and aims of individuals and groups that undertake that action.

There is a rich tradition of research investigating the psychological processes linked to collective action. Some research seeks to identify the characteristics that distinguish activists from non-activists, for example, whether activists and non-activists differ in personality characteristics (e.g., Digman, 1990). Others investigate how feelings of economic, political, or social deprivation (e.g., Relative Deprivation Theory; Runciman, 1966), or specific psychological drivers such as identification with a group and group-based anger, link to collective action (see van Zomeren, Postmes, & Spears, 2008, 2012). Sociological approaches, such as Resource Mobilisation Theory (Edwards & McCarthy, 2004; McCarthy & Zald, 1977) and the Political Process Theory (McAdam, 1982), consider the role of organisations and the political sphere in explaining how collective action actually occurs. More recently, research investigating the transition to activism has considered the extent to which particular political and cultural contexts may unlock collective action potential in individuals (e.g., van Zomeren & Louis, 2017), or set the point at which individuals decide 'enough is enough' and decide to take action (Livingstone, 2014). Perceived efficacy has been identified as a critical factor in driving motivations to engage in collective action, highlighting how the effectiveness of collective action matters both to society and to activists themselves (e.g., Klandermans & Oegema, 1987; McCarthy & Zald, 1977; van Zomeren et al., 2008, 2013).

Further, within this complex, dynamic environment, collective action involves a range of diverse individuals, each of whom may have multiple allegiances, and may engage in multiple groups with differing levels of commitment. Working together and apart, activists design and implement collective actions against a range of opponents, who in turn may or may not hold significant power to wield against them. Activists must simultaneously seek support from third parties, such as the media and other interest groups, while attempting to avoid counter-mobilisation from their opponents, and manage the challenges of radicalisation and factionalism within their own ranks. Adding to the complexity, activists for any one cause do not all share the same game plan. Some may act independently as 'lone wolves' on behalf of groups. Others may operate within highly diverse organisational structures, ranging from informal teams of friends, to loosely structured 'grassroots' organisations, to large NGOs or formal networks. These groups and structures may have differing access to resources and different abilities to use those resources to maximise the effectiveness of their activities. The larger political context also matters for collective action: activists may agitate for change within democratic and authoritarian states, where their activism may either gain support or attract repression.

How can one make sense of 'the effectiveness of collective action' in such complex and dynamic contexts? This is the question our Element seeks to answer. In this Element we focus primarily on the social psychological aspects of effective activism, although naturally we acknowledge the vital importance of other approaches, including political science, sociology, history, communication studies, and more. Given the critical role individuals play in driving the ebb and flow of broader social movements, this psychological focus may also help other disciplines seeking to understand the processes and outcomes of collective action. Our starting point is to explore 'effective' activism from the individual activist's perspective. We then consider how activists seek to influence the psychological responses of four distinct audiences: we term these audiences supporters, bystanders, opponents, and third parties.

1.1 Defining Collective Action

There are many different formulations of collective action, as it has been investigated extensively across fields spanning the natural and social sciences (e.g., see van Zomeren & Iyer, 2009; Louis et al., 2020). Collective action has been defined in social psychology as any *action aiming to improve the status, power, or influence of a group* (Wright, Taylor, & Moghaddam, 1990). A group can be any collection of two or more individuals with a shared collective identity, and thus can include a wide range of organisational structures including professional workplaces, grassroots collectives, or online communities. Individual actions, even when enacted alone, become collective through this shared goal and the individual's self-categorisation as a group member (van Zomeren & Iyer, 2009; van Zomeren & Spears, 2009). As a result, in this approach, collective action does not require a certain threshold of participants in order to count as a collective, and instead is defined by its goal of collectively solving a common problem (Wright et al., 1990).

Collective action tactics are diverse and constantly changing, ranging from marches to memes. Despite the constant and effervescent emergence of new forms of actions, scholars have put forward various typologies and subtypes to represent activists' 'action repertoires' (Sweetman et al., 2013; Tilly, 1999). Our approach within this Element is to group collective actions primarily into two types, which we contrast: *conventional actions* and *radical actions* (Moskalenko & McCauley, 2009; see also normative versus non-normative, Tausch et al., 2011; Wright, Taylor, & Moghaddam, 1990; or moderate versus militant, Louis, 2009).

The terms 'conventional' and 'radical' are subjective and what constitutes them may differ across causes and contexts (Louis et al., 2003; see also Tausch et al., 2011; Teixeira, Spears, & Yzerbyt, 2019; Wright et al., 1990). However, in general, conventional collective actions are those that follow advantaged groups' established rules or norms for civic engagement. In democratic societies, conventional actions may take the form of legal or political acts of expression and participation (e.g., signing petitions, peaceful and state-sanctioned demonstrations, and lobbying). Conversely, radical collective actions are those that violate advantaged groups' rules or norms (Louis et al., 2020; Tausch et al., 2011). Radical collective action tactics can thus include disruptive non-violent actions, illegal actions such as sabotage and civil disobedience, or violent events such as attacks and riots. However, as noted previously, the extent to which an action is considered to be conventional or radical is subjective in the eyes of the actors and the specific cause, historical period, and context (Louis, Mavor, & Terry, 2003; Louis et al., 2020).

Another central characteristic of collective action as we explore it in this Element is its *dynamic* nature. Action causes reaction, and response generates counter-response; the evaluation of these actions and responses then differs according to the particular groups and contexts involved. Activists adjust their repertoires of actions according to the audiences they seek to influence, the opportunities that arise, and the responses that they receive, sometimes working within an overarching strategy for effecting the change they seek, and sometimes choosing more impulsively or reactively (Louis, 2009; Louis et al., 2020; McCarthy & Zald, 1977; Tilly, 1999). As such, understanding effective collective action also requires understanding how actions are perceived according to the different audiences that are engaged, as well as the responses that the actions generate.

Finally, we note that there is often great *change and contestation* within activist groups (Louis, Chonu, Achia, Chapman, & Rhee, 2018; Louis et al., 2020). For many activists, as we shall see in this Element, a single collective action is just one part of a long-term strategy to achieve social change (Gulliver et al., 2019; Ulug & Acar, 2018). Accordingly, a failure may be a learning experience on the path to victory, and conversely a success is no time to relax, lest counter-mobilisation sweep away the gains achieved. As well as this constant vigilance, activists themselves undergo personal psychological trajectories as they participate in collective action over the longer term, and these internal changes affect the way that effectiveness is perceived (Drury & Reicher, 2009; Vestergren, Drury, & Chiriac, 2018; Hornsey et al., 2006).

This Element holds these central points in mind, while attempting to delve into the complexity of how effective collective action might actually be conceptualised and operationalised by activists and by researchers. This is a project that builds on many other scholars' work (e.g., Duncan, 2012; Drury & Reicher, 2000; Klandermans, 1984, 1997; Klandermans & Oegema, 1987; Louis et al., 2020; Thomas, Mavor, & McGarty, 2012; van Zomeren, Postmes, & Spears, 2008; Wright et al., 1990), and that sets out to address the spirit of the times as movements around the world seek to create profound, transformative consequences for societies (Louis, 2009; Louis & Montiel, 2018; Moghaddam, 2018; Smith, Livingstone, & Thomas, 2019).

1.2 The Following Sections

The structure of this Element is as follows. In Section 2 we will explore the notion of effective collective action and attempt the challenge of defining effective collective action in relation to specific activist audiences and time frames. In doing so, we establish a structured set of outcomes for scholars to consider, presented in two frameworks. In the subsequent four sections we then examine conceptualisations of effective activism for the four groups we have already identified: supporters, bystanders, opponents, and third parties. We review the literature (or lack of it) on effective collective action for each of these groups or targets, with an eye to identifying confirmed findings, establishing novel hypotheses, and identifying gaps. Specifically, in Section 3, we consider effective collective action for self and supporters; in Section 4, for bystanders; in Section 5, for opponents; and in Section 6, for third parties. Throughout this Element we also include examples in text boxes of effective (and ineffective) collective action taken from a range of social movements including Black Lives Matter, the far right, and the women's, peace, and environmental movements. Our goal in including these examples is to highlight how different movements have aimed to achieve effective outcomes in relation to different audiences; how the desired outcomes change in relation to the time frame envisaged; and how these outcomes are achieved within the particular social, economic, and political arenas in which they have occurred. We close with an agenda for future research and a set of key takeaways in Section 7. In this section we propose a research agenda that highlights key gaps in the literature and identifies directions for future research.

2 What Is Effective Collective Action?

One of us (Louis) is fond of telling a story from 2003, during the time of the peace rallies against the soon-to-erupt Iraq War. Louis and her office mate had both gone to the anti-war rallies in February 2003, which in Australia as elsewhere had mobilised hundreds of thousands of protestors against the imminent invasion of Iraq (Blackwood & Louis, 2012). But the huge protests failed to deter the conservative government of Australia from swiftly joining the invasion as part of the 'Coalition of the Willing'. The following month, after the war broke out and Australia was embroiled in the invasion, another protest rally was called, and Louis asked her office mate if he was going. 'No', he replied, 'I went to the rally, and it didn't work!'

This anecdote highlights the challenge of defining effective collective action. For Louis, a long-term activist, the failure of one rally to achieve peace was not a deterrent to engaging in future peace-related collective action. For her colleague, the failure of one rally identified the ineffectiveness of the action, and this lack of efficacy deterred him from engaging in future action. Their differences in aims and experiences led them to think differently about the success or failure of the collective action. In this section we expand on this point to dive into the challenges of defining what constitutes effective collective action. We then present a theoretical framework that helps to identify the diversity of goals and audiences against which effectiveness can be judged. We also consider how failure to achieve collective action goals can help to explain activist pathways towards radicalisation and towards leaving a movement, before introducing our approach to the following sections.

2.1 Defining Effective Collective Action

In this Element we define 'effectiveness' as the extent to which any one single collective action or series of such actions achieves the intended goal(s). While seemingly simple in theory, what makes this definition challenging to apply in practice is the sheer multitude of goals that individuals and groups can hold for any one collective action or sustained series of collective actions. As highlighted by our example just mentioned, these goals can range from stopping a war, to building a movement able to effect change, to feeling that you are part of something meaningful. To help structure these diverse collective action goals, researchers have highlighted three broad levels of outcome analysis: macro, meso, and micro (e.g., see van Zomeren & Iyer, 2009). Much research on collective action outcomes considers the dynamics and outcomes in the macro political–administrative context, while meso-level analysis focuses on interactions and processes at the group or organisational level. In this Element we focus primarily on micro- and meso-level analyses: the dynamics of individuals and groups. However, we acknowledge the importance of examining macro-level factors that also affect and define what social movements value and achieve (Jasper, 2004).

To help to understand effectiveness within this complex situation, we first review how individuals evaluating the effectiveness of a collective action might differ in their evaluations based on goals which are aligned to particular perceived audiences of the action, and perceived timescales for effecting change. In the case of the anti-war rally in Australia we have just highlighted, one participant's audience was the decision makers who were making the choice for the country to join the invasion of Iraq or not, and their time frame for effective change was immediate. The other participant's audience was the potential new recruits to the cause of peace activism, drawn from bystanders and third parties, and their timescale for change was long-term. Table 1 maps these diverse activist perceptions regarding the range of effective outcomes across two axes (see also Klandermans & Oegema, 1987; Oegema & Klandermans, 1994) of 'audiences' (self, supporters, bystanders, third parties, and opponents) and 'timescales' (immediate, short- to medium-term, and long-term).

Table 1 Selected effectiveness metrics for collective action audiences.

Audience	Timescale		
	Immediate	Short- and medium-term	Long-term
Self	Self-affirmation, self-empowerment, emotional experiences, meaning making, expressing loyalty and solidarity	Friendships, self-efficacy, consciousness raising, security, resources, status, sustaining action	
Supporters	Expressing group values, affirming group identities, caring, supporting, and empowering group members	Generating intentions, actions, and sustaining actions	
Bystanders	Raising awareness, building sympathy	Generating intentions and action, coalition building, avoiding counter-mobilisation	System transformation / Revolutionary change
Third parties	Raising awareness, building sympathy, creating cross-cutting identities	Generating intentions and action, coalition building, avoiding counter-mobilisation	
Opponents	Rejecting other groups' values, affirming opposition	Avoiding counter-mobilisation, initiating harm or destruction of the group, appeasing, conciliating, converting, provoking, or diverting the group	

The first and most commonly researched audience is self and supporters. Collective action directed at the self and supporters can be effective in terms of the extent to which it generates different psychological responses. These psychological responses might include enabling the expression of a group's values and identities, building identities, the generation of emotional experiences, or increasing self-efficacy perceptions. These outcomes can also be experienced as consequences of engaging in collective action. For example, collective action may be considered effective in the shorter term when it enables expressions of solidarity (i.e., directly assisting and supporting other group members and people who share a common identity), or allyship (i.e., assisting and empowering other groups; see Droogendyk, Wright, Lubensky, & Louis, 2016; Iyer & Ryan, 2009; Louis et al., 2019; McGarty, Bliuc, Thomas, & Bongiorno, 2009; Subasic, Schmitt, & Reynolds, 2011). As elaborated later, the mobilisation process, which is a key goal for supporters within the short to medium term, involves building supporters' awareness and sympathy for the cause, and eliciting concrete intentions and actions (Klandermans & Oegema, 1987; van Zomeren et al., 2008, 2012).

Turning to the longer term, another measure of effective collective action directed at the self and supporters may be the extent to which activists sustain their participation over time. Sustained collective action is critical for two reasons: first, to achieve longer-term outcomes such as policy changes over months, years, or decades; and second, simply to ensure the continuity of the group and grow the movement (Gulliver, Fielding, & Louis, 2019; Hornsey et al., 2006). Activists who sustain their participation are needed to acquire material resources, attract and support new members, and organise collective actions (e.g., see Edwards & McCarthy, 2004; McCarthy & Zald, 1977). Persisting in the face of repeated experiences of failure and rejection is also a vital challenge faced by groups (Lizzio-Wilson, Thomas, Louis, Wilcockson, Amiot, Moghaddam, & McGarty, 2021; Louis et al., 2020). Groups must manage the impact of failure both in terms of maintaining groups' existence and members' motivation to engage, but also in effectively managing the innovation process to select appropriate collective actions to leverage change over longer periods of time. Demonstrating the ability to leverage this change is also important in sustaining individuals' visions and hope for their collective future, which has been linked to willingness to take action (e.g., see Bain et al., 2013).

Beyond the self and supporters, collective action may also seek to mobilise bystanders and individuals in other interest groups ('third parties'). In this Element we distinguish between bystanders and third parties in terms of their collective identities. Bystanders are neutral observers with no known affiliation with collective action groups, whereas third parties are groups of individuals with a shared identity, who may see themselves as outside the activist group, with distinct interests, goals, and values. As a result, collective action directed towards bystanders and third parties may seek different outcomes. For bystanders, activists may seek to progress the tasks of mobilisation: raising awareness, generating sympathy for the cause, triggering intentions to engage in collective action, and eliciting actual actions (see also Louis et al., 2020). Such mobilisation efforts seek, in effect, to convert bystanders to supporters. With regard to third parties, activists may attempt a different task: to build coalitions that more narrowly seek to extend the 'chain of trust' (Louis et al., 2020) to reach and sway decision makers. More broadly, activists and third parties respond to, engage with, and co-create the social structures and norms of the wider society. For example, they respond to and participate in trends towards greater democratisation and openness, or greater authoritarianism and repression.

Finally, activists may also choose to engage opponents. Activists may seek to demobilise or convert opponents, or some factions of them, or simply seek to avoid opponents' counter-mobilisation – that is, when opponents are motivated to engage in backlash and push back (e.g., Giugni, 1998). Activists may also seek to manage opponents' radicalisation – for example, in seeking to deradicalise them. Alternatively, activists may have goals such as diverting opponents' attention, reconciling with them, or appeasing their hostility; or may have goals such as affirming rejection, shaming and stigmatising them, or even harming or destroying the opponents (Louis, Taylor, & Neil, 2004; Louis, Taylor, & Douglas, 2005).

Box 1, which considers the women's movement, also reminds us that collective action audiences and criteria of effectiveness can change as a movement advances and retreats. It also demonstrates how movements may not progress linearly, but can stagnate, jump ahead, and loop backwards as a result of dynamic events (see, e.g., Louis et al., 2020; Mundt, Ross, & Burnett, 2018). Changes in individual agency and social structures can also play an important role in understanding social change processes. For example, individuals possess

---

BOX 1 THE MANY WAVES OF THE WOMEN'S MOVEMENT

The women's rights movement (also known as the feminist movement) demonstrates how collective action goals can change over different time periods and timescales as highlighted in Table 1. The first wave, emerging in the nineteenth and early twentieth centuries in a number of Western nations, focused on obtaining full economic and political citizenship: that is, gaining the right for women to vote, and eliminating barriers to opportunities in education and employment (e.g., Ferree & Mueller 2004). In this early wave, organised activism used a diverse collective action repertoire including rallies as well as disruptive action. Over the following decades, the movement became international and grew in both size and strength, increasing the supporter base and building alliances. The second wave occurred in the context of the broader social revolution during the 1960s and 1970s. This wave sought to increase women's inclusion in politics, but also addressed a range of other issues including working conditions, family obligations, and sexuality (Paxton, Hughes, & Green, 2006). The third wave (from the mid-1990s) moved from citizenship and inclusion to advocating for targets for women's representation, whether through gender quotas or laws (Paxton et al., 2006). More recently, some scholars have identified a fourth wave of feminism, heralded online through hashtags such as #MeToo, which both argues for the inclusion of more diverse voices, and promotes sharing of experiences of normalised, everyday sexism (e.g., Munro, 2013).

While the narrative of movement waves may imply a progression in goals and achievements, researchers highlight, however, that each wave has focused on different audiences while also navigating counter-mobilisation and dissenting voices. This process has set contested parameters around who was included in the movement and who was not, and also achieved substantial gains while negotiating internal disagreement and external discrimination (e.g., Lizzio-Wilson, Masser, Hornsey, & Iyer, 2020).

different elements of agency – that is, different capacity and capabilities to act, which are linked to social structures that are incrementally changing around us (May, 2011). The war is not the battle: an event may fail in the short term but still progress the broader agenda, enhance individuals' agency, alter social structures, or slow the pace or likelihood of a looming defeat.

Taken together, the diversity of goals in Table 1 reminds us that social change requires long-term collective action. As such, better understanding these individual and group-level dynamics is critical to any analysis of the social psychology of effective collective action.

2.2 Frameworks for Conceptualisations of Effectiveness and Failure

As Table 1 suggests, the perceived aims and effectiveness of a movement or an action depend upon the eye of the beholder. As a result, in the present Element we seek to identify the shared psychological processes which individuals experience when responding to, and engaging in, collective action broadly. We propose two frameworks that may be useful for a new scholarship of dynamic collective action. Specifically, we propose a framework for understanding effectiveness in relation to collective action audiences across two subsets of tasks: mobilising individuals, and persisting to power (the ABIASCA framework). Following this, we then turn our attention to how activists may respond to collective action failure, and present a second model, DIME.

2.3 A Framework for Understanding Effectiveness in Different Tasks: ABIASCA

Our framework was inspired by the work of Klandermans and Oegema (1987), who reviewed key factors that had prevented people from mobilising in a peace campaign for a rally within a particular Dutch community. These authors identified four barriers to engaging in collective action: lack of awareness of the campaign; lack of sympathy with the goals of the movement; not having formed an intention to act; and not implementing their intentions (Figure 1).

Klandermans and Oegema's (1987) analysis suggests a series of tasks that activists need to undertake as they seek to mobilise people, from addressing ignorance or opposition through to encouraging attitude and behaviour change. These tasks include awareness raising, building sympathy, turning sympathy into intentions, and turning intentions into actions. In the present model, we adopt this framework to propose that progressing individuals through these tasks is required to effectively *mobilise* individuals in collective action regardless of which audience they may be in: self, supporters, bystanders, third parties, or even opponent groups.

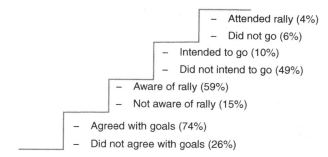

Figure 1 Klandermans and Oegema's (1987) analysis of community engagement with a peace rally in the Netherlands.

The second component of our model identifies the tasks required to 'persist to power' – a term we use to convey the actions that produce the desired externally realised outcomes and sustain them in the face of opposition. That is, groups must sustain their activism over time, form coalitions with parties outside their present supporters, and avoid counter-mobilising opponents. In recognition of the many steps required to achieve system change, many activists create interim success criteria around movement building (e.g., Hornsey et al., 2006; Uluğ & Acar, 2018). We connect this second group of tasks back to the goals of longer-term collective action identified in Table 1 (see also Thomas et al., 2019; Thomas & McGarty, 2018; Thomas, Rathmann, & McGarty, 2017). Figure 2 groups the seven tasks we identify within each of these two components: mobilising individuals, and persisting to power. The framework, like Table 1, is not intended to be exhaustive, but to invite scholars' consideration of the diversity of aims that social movement actors juggle, for the various audiences they may be oriented to, and therefore the dimensions or metrics on which effectiveness and success (or failure) can be evaluated by activists and others.

What we aim to argue in this Element and to unpack in the next four sections is that activists may seek to achieve different goals and tasks for different audiences. The degree to which collective action is effective thus depends upon the activists themselves and the supporters they may be trying to mobilise; the bystanders they may be trying to inform and engage; the third parties whose attention must be captured and whose assistance and support is invited; and the opponents whom the actors are hoping to overcome.

2.4 Failure Diversifies Movements: The DIME Model

While sustained collective action may be required to achieve long-term change, each unique collective action generates its own psychological response and counter-response. Some forms of collective action, such as holding market

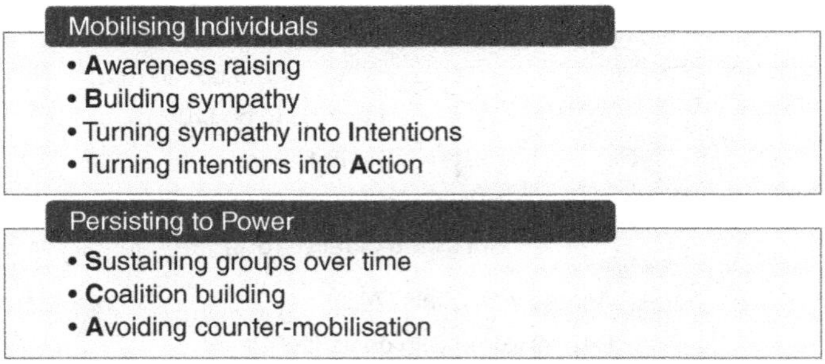

Figure 2 The ABIASCA framework: mapping collective action effectiveness.

stalls or organising information nights, might be designed around goals such as raising awareness and generating sympathy in bystanders. Petitions may be organised to increase a group's supporter base, or to prompt the attention and favourable responses of third parties. The list of possible actions is vast: Sharp (1973) distinguished nearly 200 forms of non-violent activist tactics, from sit-ins to street theatre, and others have updated and expanded the list (e.g., Beer, 2021). Some of these actions also may have in mind multiple audiences, while others may be oriented to different audiences at different times. For example, collective action using street theatre may seek to generate bystander awareness and media attention, while a sit-in may be designed to disrupt a specific targeted business.

The experience and commitment of activists, and their orientation to the short- or longer-term time frames, are not just important in their selection of particular ABIASCA tasks and audiences to focus on. Such considerations also matter when we consider more narrowly how activists will respond to failure and defeat. For example, by definition, long-term activists must succeed in sustaining motivation in the face of delay and lost battles; to do so, they may downplay the dimensions on which any one specific collective action 'failed', while psychologically emphasising the ways in which the collective action 'succeeded' (Blackwood & Louis, 2012). Multiple voices may also attempt to address the question of whether a movement is succeeding or failing: committed activists may be more dismissive of failure signals from outsiders or authorities, and more responsive to encouraging messages about success from movement leaders, allowing the activists to sustain their participation in the movement despite any setbacks and disappointments they encounter (Lizzio-Wilson et al., 2021).

Activists may also vary in their theories of change, whether informal ('Think globally, act locally'), or formal, such as Macy's (2007) theory of 'the great turning' in the environmental movement, or the political process

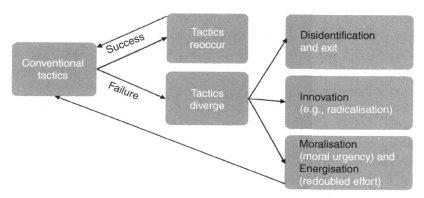

Figure 3 The DIME model, proposing that failure prompts activists to diverge towards disidentification, innovation, moralisation, and energisation.

model (McAdam, 1982). Formal theories of change identify recommended tactics, and chart milestones along the proposed paths to eventual triumph. But whether formal or informal, to the extent that different activists have different theories of change, we would expect them to have different notions of the practical steps needed to grow their groups' effectiveness and build towards their ultimate victories. Consequently their judgements of effectiveness will vary in line with these formal or informal ideas of how social transformation occurs.

To better understand how activists may respond to failure, we put forward a second model, the DIME model, for consideration and empirical testing (Lizzio-Wilson et al., 2021; Louis et al., 2020). A dime, as not all readers may know, is a ten-cent coin in some Western currencies. The coin is generally small, and in English, the expressions to 'stop on a dime' and 'turn on a dime' both indicate abrupt changes of direction and pace. With the DIME model (Figure 3; see Louis et al., 2020) we attempted to consider the volatility of collective action, and specifically to theorise the diversifying impact of failure on activists.

As Figure 3 illustrates, the DIME model proposes that while success would often lead to persistence in the original tactics, failure would diversify activists, leading to separate groups, who show different trajectories. Some actors, in the face of failure, would show _Disidentification,_ losing commitment and sometimes exiting a group. A second set of activists might show _Moralisation_, greater moral urgency and conviction, and _Energisation_, a desire to ramp up the pace and intensity of the existing tactics. As a result when faced with failure, this group would double down on their initial choices. And finally, a third group of activists might show _Innovation_ of tactics, introducing new types of action (including both radicalisation and deradicalisation) in an effort to see the group succeed. Of course, the same activist might show all three of these responses at different points in time, or in different causes that they were engaged in, but for any one defeat, in the DIME model we imagine that divergent trajectories would form for subgroups within the movement.

In one initial test of the impact of failure on activists' trajectories (Lizzio-Wilson et al., 2021), we used the context of a plebiscite vote in Australia on gay marriage to follow proponents and opponents of the change before, immediately after, and three months after the vote was held. Before the vote, latent class analysis distinguished two subgroups within both supporters and opponents of gay marriage: essentially, these corresponded to moderate and keen advocates for each side. After the vote (which proponents of gay marriage won), supporters homogenised into a dominant class accounting for 97 per cent of the sample, with moderate intentions to continue to support change. In contrast, opponents differentiated into groups which persisted over time, and varied in the degree of their resignation, intentions to continue with conventional tactics, and desire for innovation.

2.5 Where to from Here?

The ABIASCA and DIME frameworks, as just highlighted, both point to the reality that *activists have a diversity of potential tasks and audiences to engage.* Definitions of success or failure and conceptualisations of effectiveness therefore often hinge on different orientations to particular tasks for particular audiences in particular time frames. In addition, whether a rebuff given by the authorities is a crushing defeat that spurs abandonment of the movement, or a last-ditch effort by a failing power that spurs further confident action, or a prompt to radicalisation, is often hotly contested by factions and groups within any broader social movement.

As our two frameworks suggest, then, defining effective collective action requires understanding activists' contested perceptions of three collective action elements: the collective action audience, the timescale for evaluating effectiveness, and the specific goals or tasks that the collective action is meant to achieve. With those points in mind, the next sections will review the literature (or lack thereof) on how activists seek to elicit different outcomes from each of these different audiences (illustrated in Figure 4).

3 Self and Supporters

The literature that is reviewed in this section is the heart of social psychological research on collective action: research studying the motives and mobilisation of

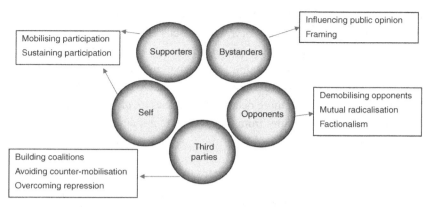

Figure 4 Collective action audiences and example effectiveness measures.

activists themselves. This is perhaps unsurprising: activists are the most visible and critical component of any social movement. As a result, the research has often focused on them, and has identified consistent aspects of activists' beliefs and perceptions that are linked to their collective action intentions and behaviours. Thus, an important starting point in any consideration of the social psychology of effective activism is to consider what factors increase these individuals' short- and long-term mobilisation intentions.

One critical aspect of the mobilisation of supporters is their social identity, examined in social identity and self-categorisation theories (Tajfel & Turner, 1979; Turner et al., 1987). Social Identity Theory proposes that individuals have both a sense of themselves as individuals ('I', the personal identity), and as groups ('we', the social identities). Each individual is a member of a variety of groups, including those defined by social categories (e.g., nation, ethnicity, religion, gender, etc.) and also groups defined by shared opinions or actions as supporters or opponents of particular causes (Bliuc et al., 2003; McGarty et al., 2009). Particular identities become more salient in contexts that highlight greater similarities (e.g., of experience, values, attitudes, and actions) among group members, and greater differences from other groups. Identity salience matters, because when people identify as members of a group, they will see others group members' experiences as relevant to them; they will be more likely to care about other group members; they will be more likely to align with the social rules or norms of the group; and they will be more likely to take collective action for the group.

A focus on activists' social identities therefore invites researchers to understand activists as members of groups, both formal and informal. In the following sections, we focus on three ABIASCA steps for supporters of a particular cause: turning sympathy into intentions, turning intentions into action, and sustaining activism to persist over time. We thus start our analysis (as much of the literature has done) in the middle of the story, with a focus on individuals who already have awareness of a cause, and are presumed to have sympathy for it. Our focus in this section is important: turning the passive awareness and sympathy of supporters into action is critical for effective collective action. In Section 4, on bystanders, we consider in more detail the processes involved in raising awareness and generating sympathy from those who are not already members of the supporter group.

3.1 Turning Sympathy into Intentions

Group norms and identities, as well as individual differences, are key to turning sympathy for a cause into intentions to engage in collective action. At the group level, the most critical factors are the groups' norms (their social rules or standards for appropriate behaviour), which play a vital role in determining when a baseline level of sympathy for a cause will turn into action (Terry, Hogg, & White, 1999; Turner, Hogg, Oakes, Reicher, & Wetherell, 1987). When people take on a social identity as a member of a group, they adopt its norms, which may support collective action in some cases, but in other cases may actively inhibit it. While all groups have unique constellations of norms for action and inaction, a general pattern that is observed is that groups are more likely to have norms supporting collective action to address the grievances and concerns that afflict their own group members. Put differently, one reason why intentions might not form for collective action given sympathy for a cause is if people do not take responsibility for the suffering of others who are not within their psychologically salient in-group: a social identity linked to an advantaged group does not necessarily come with norms to help the disadvantaged (e.g., Louis et al., 2019). In such cases, passive and remote expressions of sympathy might be the 'action' that is offered.

However, even when activists identify as members of groups that share experiences of suffering, this is not enough to create an imperative to act in the group's interest, according to Social Identity Theory (Tajfel & Turner, 1979). Beliefs about the status quo matter: it is when groups believe that the status quo is illegitimate or unjust, and that it has the potential to change (instability), that collective action is more likely to emerge. In an important contribution to this literature, van Zomeren and colleagues (2008) reviewed sixty-nine published studies on the social psychology of collective action, and used their meta-analysis to construct a new Social Identity Model of Collective Action (SIMCA: van Zomeren et al., 2004, 2008, 2013). In SIMCA, support for collective action is predicted from four focal variables: social identity, group efficacy, group-based emotions, and moral conviction. The first of these, social identity, refers to the individual's psychological sense of belonging to a particular group (Turner et al., 1987). Identity is the key psychological variable driving collective action, and is associated with action directly as well as through indirect paths. For example, identification as an environmental activist predicts intentions to engage in environmental activism (Fielding, McDonald, & Louis, 2008; see also Fielding & Hornsey, 2016), and recent longitudinal research within the SIMCA framework has provided further evidence for the central role of identity in motivating collective action (Thomas, Zubielevitch, Sibley, & Osborne, 2020).

Identity also drives action via two other paths, the first being via anger, and specifically group-based anger such as might arise from perceptions of collective disadvantage and injustice (van Zomeren et al., 2004; see also Leach, Iyer, & Pedersen, 2006). When we identify with a group experiencing injustice, we get angry, and we form an intention to do something about it.

A second instrumental path is via perceived effectiveness or efficacy: the belief that one's group has the capacity to effect the desired change (see also, Bandura, 2000; Klandermans, 1984). When we identify with a group and we think there's a concrete way of taking action to meet our group's goals, we form an intention to act.

Moral conviction is the fourth focal variable, which has been included in more recent SIMCA research (van Zomeren, 2013; van Zomeren, Postmes, & Spears, 2012). Moral conviction refers to a strong and absolute stance based on the appraisal that the issue is a moral issue, and it is theorised to act both as a distal motivator for identification and collective action more broadly (van Zomeren, 2013), and as a direct predictor alongside or in interaction with considerations of injustice or efficacy (e.g., Alberici & Milesi, 2016; Louis et al., 2020; Thomas, Mavor, & McGarty, 2012). Of course, these emotions and efficacy beliefs are not just specific to one individual decision-maker: groups talk and think together to understand and process what their group's position is and what should be done (Thomas & McGarty, 2009).

Another way of understanding the transformation of an identity to become associated with norms supporting collective action is that identity must become *politicised* (Simon & Grabow, 2010; Simon & Klandermans, 2001). According to this line of work, an identity associated with collective action intentions will include a perception of shared grievances, attributed to a distinct cause such as an enemy, or a sense of injustice and group-based emotions such as anger (e.g., see Rees & Bamberg, 2014). These perceptions are then transformed into collective norms, for action perceived as effective (e.g., see Fritsche et al., 2018).

Politicised identities are formed through group discussion and interaction, as individuals adopt normative perceptions of the need for action, come to feel shared emotions and moral urgency, and jointly come to define the situation as one in which it is appropriate and efficacious to act (Smith, Thomas, & McGarty, 2015; Thomas et al., 2012). Box 2 discusses how the Internet can be used to turn emotions such as anger that are socially shared into identities that flow on to intentions. In turn, engagement in collective action can further transform group members' social identities into more politicised identities, when it consolidates activists' participation in the normative consensus that there is injustice, which is outrageous and morally wrong, and which we can do something about (Drury & Reicher, 2000, 2005, 2009; Thomas et al., 2012; van Zomeren et al., 2008).

Politicised identity has been shown to be consistently linked to political beliefs, policy support, and activism – for example, regarding anthropogenic causes of climate change (Unsworth & Fielding, 2014). However, identity can also negatively impact supporters' participation. For example, negative stereotypes about environmental activists have been linked to disidentification and political inaction among those who sympathise with environmentalism (Stuart, Thomas, & Donaghue, 2018). The factors identified in the SIMCA model, along with norms and injustice, have been studied by many scholars of collective action who focus on group processes and intergroup relations.

Turning to individual-level factors that generate intentions, other psychological characteristics such as empathy and perspective taking have also been shown to play a role. Empathy has the potential to promote collective action by facilitating sympathy for others' grievances (Zak & Barraza, 2013). Empathy can also help to consolidate the link to intentions and action by rewarding those who do engage in action with the relief of distress (e.g., Bowles & Gintis, 2011). There are other possibilities, however, including that empathic distress would lead some individuals to actively avoid news of injustice and suffering, or promote endorsement of immediate symbolic gestures ('thoughts and prayers') rather than more effortful long-term action that might force the actors to sit longer with their discomfort (Klimecki & Singer, 2012).

In addition to empathy, a number of studies on support for collective action have considered the extent to which the 'Big Five' personality traits play a role in generating intentions to engage in collective action (i.e., Openness, Conscientiousness, Extraversion, Agreeableness, and Neuroticism; Digman, 1990; McCrae & Costa, 1987). Individuals' higher open-mindedness and enjoyment of trying new things is associated with political engagement (Gallego & Oberski, 2012; Gerber, Huber, Doherty, & Dowling, 2011). In contrast, people who have higher neuroticism (which is the tendency to experience negative emotions more intensely) and agreeableness (meaning sociability and a desire for harmony)

Box 2 Black Lives Matter: Turning Sympathy into Intentions Online

The Internet provides the opportunity for activists to reach a greater number of potential supporters – for example, using memes and emotional images to inform people, frame issues, and shape attitudes towards political action (e.g., Leach & Allen, 2017). The Black Lives Matter (BLM) movement itself was sparked by the hashtag #BlackLivesMatter after the acquittal of George Zimmerman for the shooting death of Trayvon Martin in 2012. Another hashtag related to the movement, #Ferguson, became the most used social-issue hashtag in the ten years from 2006 to 2016 (Anderson & Hitlin, 2016).

From the perspective of this Element's ABIASCA framework, the widespread dissemination of internet hashtags can be understood to function both to raise awareness and to grow sympathy. In addition, awareness and sympathy that are expressed collectively will build an identity around support for a cause, which then may mobilise sympathisers to turn their favourable attitudes into concrete intentions and actions. Hashtag activism can thus be an effective strategy (see also Thomas et al., 2015) in creating the foundations needed for mobilisation and 'persistence to power'. For example, Pew Social Trends found that two-thirds of American adults support the #BLM movement, including majorities of White (60 per cent), Hispanic (77 per cent), and Asian (75 per cent) American respondents (Parker, Horowitz, & Anderson, 2020).

tend to avoid involvement in political action, perhaps because conflict and confrontation are experienced more negatively (Gerber et al., 2011; Ha, Kim, & Jo, 2013). In addition, conscientiousness is associated with greater willingness to engage in political action when the action is perceived as a duty (Gallego & Oberski, 2012; Gerber et al., 2011). The consideration of individual differences in personality factors such as these is an important direction of future research.

3.2 Turning Intentions into Action

Social psychological research outside collective action (such as in the health domain) has intensively considered the processes involved in turning intentions into behaviour. This research has demonstrated how 'volitional constructs' – such as implementation intentions to achieve a goal – are positively associated with taking action (e.g., Gollwitzer & Sheeran, 2006). However, in the collective action context, it must be acknowledged that social psychology research focuses primarily on predictors of intentions to engage in collective action, despite widespread calls to include behavioural measures in studies (e.g.,

Bamberg et al., 2015; 2020). While there are nuances that we will review later, it is also the case that activists may be deterred from forming or enacting intentions by risks, particularly in the face of more repressive and/or violent possible responses from the state (e.g., Davenport, 2000, 2007).

3.3 Action over Time: Sustaining Persistent Engagement in Collective Action

Raising awareness, generating sympathy, and motivating action are all important outcomes of effective collective action. However, these outcomes often depend upon the organisational structures available and the persistence (or lack thereof) of particular activists. The organisation of collective action may be undertaken by social movement groups, offline or online, with formal or grassroots organisational structures. Given that many collective action groups depend on volunteers, the burdens of sustained engagement might be high (e.g., Gulliver et al., 2020). In this context, it is important to acknowledge the importance of longstanding volunteers, who play a critical role in maintaining social movement organisations (Baggetta, Han, & Andrews, 2013; Curtin & McGarty, 2016). Persistent activists are needed to take on organisational or leadership roles, allowing the acquisition of resources to sustain the group, and coordination of actions (Carman & Nesbit, 2013; Edwards & McCarthy, 2004).

Given the importance to a cause of activists who persist over time, we now review what the scholarship shows as predictors of sustained activism. While the comparative absence of longitudinal research has been noted by many, unsurprisingly stronger activist identification, along with stronger social and organisational links, have been shown to be significant predictors of persistent engagement in activism (e.g., Louis et al., 2016; McAdam, 1982). In addition, factors such as available time may play a critical role. For example, Downton and Wehr (1998) found that peace activists with flexible careers and no children sustained greater engagement in collective action over time.

Another factor is the impact of the action upon the activists themselves. Some scholars have demonstrated that engaging in collective action has enduring psychological consequences for individuals (Drury & Reicher, 2005; Vestergren et al., 2018) as well as profound, transformative consequences for societies (Louis, 2009; Louis & Montiel, 2018; Moghaddam, 2018; Smith, Livingstone, & Thomas, 2019). While research on the psychological motivations of persistent activists remains comparatively neglected, studies have suggested that symbolic and identity-affirming aspects of collective action can play an important role in reinforcing sustained engagement in collective action, allowing ongoing participation even when the achievement of social change remains a distant dream. For example, Hornsey and colleagues (2006) identified that perceived effectiveness of activism in expressing one's values was associated with intentions to persist in activism over time (see also Gusfield, 1986). LGBTIQ+ and Black pride action, or religious collective action, often utilises mobilisation to affirm in-group values and identities as a core component of many campaigns.

Some forms of collective action, or orientations to activism, may be easier to sustain than others due to their different motivations. Allyship, for example, involves helping a group perceived to be distinct or different, and can be motivated by a desire to enact one's own group's values or to secure its political interests (Droogendyk et al., 2016; Iyer & Ryan, 2009; Louis et al., 2019). This values-based motive for allyship may be easier to sustain over time. Similarly, other actions may be perceived as effective just by being carried out. These include benevolent acts which aim to express solidarity with a specific disadvantage or harm, in contrast with collective actions that are oriented towards system transformation (Thomas, Rathmann, & McGarty, 2017) or system support (Jost, Becker, Osborne, & Badaan, 2017). These acts of solidarity allow the actors to affirm their identities and experiences together. In these contexts, collective action may be more easily sustained (Blackwood & Louis, 2012).

Turning to emotional outcomes, it is the case that for some activists, participation in collective action may itself be energising, creating a joyful sense of collective effervescence which is intrinsically meaningful and rewarding (Drury & Reicher, 2005; Hopkins et al., 2016; Thomas et al., 2012). To experience heightened solidarity and collective effervescence may represent outcomes which are ends in themselves for some activists. For others, as we have noted, symbolic and emotional outcomes may have value to the extent that they also build an identity that feeds forward to sustain long-term activism.

Without positive emotional or symbolic rewards for persistent activism, many researchers have noted high rates of burnout among activists over time (Chen & Gorski, 2015). Burnout is a condition where activists halt their activities and lose their psychological drive to continue in their work (Freudenberger, 1974). It is a correlate of disidentification and exit from the movement, which we briefly discussed in relation to the DIME model in Section 2, but also implies poor well-being outcomes for the activists. Burnout is costly to activist groups, because the loss of persistent activists both reduces the groups' capacity to organise collective action in the present and reduces the pool of leaders and organisers for the future. Activists' burnout has been associated with the burden of witnessing suffering and oppression (Goodwin & Pfaff, 2001), as well as low resources and public apathy (Gomes, 1992), and negative relationships with other activists (Hopgood, 2006). Burnout and dropout of system-change-oriented activists is common (Blackwood & Louis, 2012), which may be no surprise given the high bar set for effectiveness when transformative system change is the goal.

In addition to the importance of identity affirmation in sustaining activism already noted, demobilising effects of failure are anticipated in DIME (Louis et al., 2020), such that for some activists, the perceived ineffectiveness of one past action may lead to disidentification with the movement and lower intentions to engage in future actions. This lower perceived efficacy and the inability to sustain intentions in the face of setbacks may be more common among those who were less strongly committed to or identified with the movement in the first place (e.g., Blackwood & Louis, 2012; Lizzio-Wilson et al., 2021). In addition, we propose that such disengagement may be more common among those who do not *innovate* in response to setbacks over time. As Box 3 highlights, movements that persist through the decades required to achieve social transformation may thrive as much through activists' innovation and their diverse responses to new opportunities and setbacks, as through the continuing existence of particular groups and organisations over time to address the originally mapped grievances and goals. Here leadership may play a role: leaders' call to persistence rather than throwing in the towel in the face of setbacks is a cue that many group members will explicitly respond to (e.g., Blackwood & Louis, 2017). Leaders, too, are important in establishing organisational climates of inclusiveness, support, and positivity, which also have been associated with group members' persistence in activism (e.g., Hopgood, 2006). Given the importance of persistent activists in organising and leading collective action, increased attention in future research to the factors that allow activists to persist and to avoid burnout will be of great value.

4 Bystanders

In this Element, we use the term bystanders to refer to those who have not decided either to support or to oppose a particular activist cause. There are a number of reasons why bystanders can influence the outcomes of collective action. First, given the attrition of activists over time that we have just discussed (see also Klandermans, 1997), recruitment of bystanders can be helpful or even necessary to reinvigorate and sustain ongoing collective action over time. As a broader point, however, bystander responses may influence public opinion and political support for the cause. If we refer back to Table 1 in Section 2, we see that activists may engage in a diverse array of tasks for the bystander audience: in the shorter term, awareness raising and building sympathy, and in the longer

Box 3 Changing Organisations in the Australian Environmental Movement

The Australian environmental movement serves as a case study of effective sustained action; as a whole, the movement has survived and sustained collective action for more than 150 years. As the detailed case study provided by Gulliver, Fielding, and Louis (2020) also illustrates, consistent with the ABIASCA framework, one aspect of the persistence of the movement is that a diversity and sequence of goals and tasks have been engaged in by environmental activists over time.

Beginning with groups such as the Field Naturalists' Society of South Australia (formed 1883) and Birds Australia (formed 1905), early environmentalists' primary goals were to undertake surveys and species expeditions, and lobby for the creation of National Parks for the preservation of these threatened species. After a string of National Parks were designated, Australian environmental organisations began to seek protection for urban wilderness (lobbying for the 'Green Bans' of the 1970s) and for regional forests threatened by logging and development (e.g., the Terrania Creek and Franklin Blockades). In the next wave of the movement, more than 6,000 Landcare and Bushcare groups were formed, aiming to restore lands degraded by agriculture and industry. Most recently, since the turn of the century, there has been an explosion of new climate- and sustainability-focused groups. Contemporary activists demand 'climate justice', and action to address climate change. New participants in the movement include groups building community resilience in a carbon-constrained world (e.g., Transition Town groups), and groups calling for the reintegration of Indigenous knowledge into the management of Australia's environment (e.g., Firesticks Alliance). Since 2010 alone, almost 500 groups have organised more than 36,000 collective action events, the majority of which are undertaken by groups dependent on volunteers.

term, mobilising bystanders to act, and minimising bystander counter-mobilisation.

In the present section, we first consider techniques that activists can use to raise awareness and develop sympathy among bystanders, investigating the literature on agenda setting and public opinion. We then turn to the scholarship on the importance of framing when communicating with bystanders, pausing to highlight effective and ineffective mobilising frames. While this literature is well established, bringing bystanders over to the cause may also bring new perils; we examine the scholarship on these challenges in detail in the final portion of this section.

4.1 Raising Awareness and Developing Sympathy among Bystanders

To some it might seem intuitive that if people are aware of a problem or injustice, their sympathy will naturally be evoked and action naturally follows. However, as we have already seen in Section 3, this is not always the case (see also Small, Loewenstein, & Slovic, 2007). Mere awareness of a problem, in short, will not necessarily lead to solution-focused action. So what will? We employ the ABIASCA framework reviewed in Section 2 to identify that effective mobilisation requires that activists must move bystanders from awareness to sympathy, concrete intentions to act, and actual actions.

4.2 Agenda Setting, Public Opinion, and Perceived Relevance

To the extent that activists are thinking of bystanders as a target audience, a critical challenge they face is often simply raising awareness of the cause or injustice that needs to be addressed. As we have just seen, awareness is not the end of the story – but it is surely an important beginning. The challenge of awareness raising may be interpreted with the assistance of the literature on public opinion (Glynn & Huge, 2008; Lippman, 1922), which studies the views or attitudes of publics with regard to topics of the day, including how public opinion is formed and what its impact is. One of the key messages in the public opinion literature is that democratic policymakers are responsive to what the public wants (Burstein, 1998, 2003). For this reason alone, it is clear that activists will seek to have an impact on public opinion. The literature on agenda setting (e.g., Dearing, Rogers, & Rogers, 1996) adds to this critical message by highlighting two further factors important to activists: that public opinion is responsive to media coverage, and that when an issue or concern is covered by the media, politicians become more willing to carry out what the public wants (Burstein, 2003). We return to both of these topics in Section 6 (which focuses on collective action and third parties, including the media and decision makers), but for the purposes of the present discussion, we note that activists who are facing the challenge of capturing public opinion often seek to elicit media coverage.

What does it mean to capture public opinion? As we have seen and will elaborate in the next section, awareness-raising goals encompass increased awareness of a topic (such as carbon emissions) as well as awareness of facts that generate sympathy for one's own point of view (e.g., that carbon emissions will create devastating climate change) and awareness of facts that generate intentions to act (e.g., that carbon emissions can be reduced by particular concrete steps, such as ending fossil fuel subsidies). Mere intellectual awareness of a topic itself is not usually the aim of activists. Rather, activists face the challenge of conveying information that leads to the view that a particular topic is relevant to the bystanders' lives, and that there are reasons for sympathy and action.

4.3 Framing to Increase Awareness and Sympathy among Bystanders

Activists meet the challenge of eliciting sympathy and action by meaning making, or framing: 'to select some aspects of a perceived reality and make them more salient in a communication . . . in such a way as to promote a particular problem definition, causal interpretation, moral evaluation, and/or treatment recommendation for the item described' (Entman, 1993, p. 52). Framing occurs in media representations and leaders' rhetoric (Goffman, 1974; Weaver, 2007), but is also a central concern in collective action (Benford & Snow, 2000; Gamson, Fireman, & Rytina, 1982; Klandermans, 1997; Snow & Benford, 1988). Specific tasks that activists' frames must accomplish include:

(1) identifying problems (diagnosis)
(2) identifying an alternative or solution
(3) mobilising others to act together to implement the solution

For the purposes of the present Element, the framing tasks are clearly linked to the ABIASCA projects of building awareness and sympathy, intentions, and actions. According to framing scholars, particular frames will be more persuasive in mobilising audiences when they are consistent internally, supported by reality, and shared by credible sources (e.g., Benford & Snow, 2000). Yet, empirically, activists often fail to create a compelling frame around their problem. Disagreement among collective action organisations often erupts about the appropriate frame, such that activists do not communicate clearly what is happening, who is responsible, and what the next steps should be (Benford & Snow, 2000; Klandermans et al., 1999; Klandermans & Oegema, 1987). This confusion is a factor not just in recruitment and retention of new activists, but also in the outcomes of collective action: robust diagnostic frames and solution frames are also associated with movement effectiveness (Cress & Snow, 2000).

The early minority influence literature also identifies elements of persuasive communication of frames that activists will benefit from as they seek to mobilise others: consistency and confidence (Moscovici, Lage, & Naffrechoux, 1969), and apparent public spirit, which may also be evidenced by willingness to endure hardship (Maass, Clark, & Haberkorn, 1982). The perception of momentum or growth in support for a frame is also a factor that can facilitate influence (Gordijn, de Vries, & de Dreu, 2002). In contrast, a diversity of frames, communicated by actors with apparent vested interests, or frames that do not identify a clear problem, a chain of responsibility, or a clear opportunity to act, are all much less likely to sway bystanders' decisions. Yet it is extremely common for different factions of a movement to compete for bystanders' attention, each putting forward different frames for the way forward (Thomas & Louis, 2013; see also Box 4). Militant and moderate wings, lobbyists and activists, left- and right-wing parties may put forward different regional, national, and international visions relating to the same issue. Choosing among such frames is no easy task.

One attribute that may be important in making a frame more compelling is whether a frame claims injustice or not. Gamson (1992) boldly argued that 'collective action frames are injustice frames' (p. 68), and as we saw in Section 3, it is clear that communicating that injustice has occurred is focal to many activists' frames and to effective mobilisation (van Zomeren, 2013; van Zomeren et al., 2004, 2008). As we have also noted in Section 3, another element of effective framing is a clear depiction of the effectiveness of action: its efficacy. Compelling communications about both injustice and efficacy, in turn, often rest on compelling communication of shared identities, and communication that the collective action is supported by shared group norms (Jasper, 1997; Louis, 2009; Louis et al., 2020; Turner et al., 1987).

The creation of a shared identity to mobilise has been explored compellingly by Reicher, Haslam, and colleagues in their literature on identity entrepreneurship (Haslam, Reicher, & Platow, 2010; Reicher, Cassidy, Wolpert, Hopkins, & Levine, 2006; Steffens, Haslam, Ryan, & Kessler, 2013). As we have just seen, political communication from various groups, leaders, and activists presents frames that seek to capture attention and shape responses (Bennett & Iyengar, 2008; McNair, 2017). Box 5 discusses such framing challenges in relation to environmental movements. These normative messages about the social rules or standards for attitudes and actions are more persuasive when the norms are seen to characterise a common group that people care about or identify with. If a message is put forward about a particular action by a group, people who care about or identify with the group will take the message on board to the extent that it is seen as in line with the group's norms; they will then internalise the normative attitudes, and enact the normative behaviours. Thus leaders and advocates who communicate *who we are* – how the behaviour flows from the identity and norms of the group – will be most able to mobilise audiences.

Yet people who care about a group are also more committed to the values and aims or interests of a group (Louis, Taylor, & Douglas, 2005). They are

Box 4 Frames for the Far Right, Voting Behaviour, and Radicalisation

Far right groups form a diverse and loosely connected network who seek to promote extreme nationalism, authoritarianism, xenophobia, and Islamophobia (e.g., Caiani & Della Porta, 2018). Far right frames identify foreigners (especially Muslims) as a problem that European societies face; strong borders and ethnic definitions of citizenship as solutions; and strong leaders who enact traditional values as the means to achieve these ends. Under the umbrella term of the 'far right', however, two different wings of the movement have been identified (Golder, 2016): the radical right, which is not directly opposed to democracy, and the extreme right, which sees democracy as part of the problem, and seeks to replace it with neo-fascism.

The difference in frames has had important implications. Countries such as Germany have banned extremist parties but tolerated other far right parties (Mudde, 2007). Far right activity in the electoral arena has achieved significant gains in gaining support from bystanders and influencing voting behaviour (Gattinara & Pirro, 2019). The effectiveness of far right parties is evidenced by participation in coalition and minority governments in European countries such as Austria, Switzerland, and Bulgaria, and the gaining of influence in other countries such as France and Hungary (Golder, 2016). Applying the ABIASCA model, it appears that the radical wing of the far right movement has been effective in the tasks of converting sympathy into voting intentions and behaviour.

However, among banned extremist groups, failure to gain electoral power may have influenced the trajectory towards extreme right violence (see also Gattinara & Pirro, 2019). The DIME model (Section 2; Louis et al., 2020) suggests that activists turn to more radical tactics in part as alternatives after the failure of conventional forms of collective action. Consistent with this interpretation, Muis and Immerzeel (2017) found that the more effective the European radical right was in gaining an electoral foothold, the less radical their protest activities became (but see Jackle & Konig, 2017).

therefore – at least sometimes – more attentive to discrepancies between a group's actual and ideal norms, and more likely to emerge as activists, leaders, or dissidents (Dupuis, Wohl, Packer, & Tabri, 2016; Packer, 2009). Such public-spirited activists are important, because to the extent that such advocates are seen as embodying the group's values and committed to its interests, they are more likely to exert influence (Haslam et al., 2010; Steffens

BOX 5 ENVIRONMENTAL ADVOCACY AND FRAMING

The environmental movement engages in campaigns in order to disseminate information about an issue and prompt calls to action. Environmental communication campaigns (ECCs) differ from other forms of environmental communication seeking merely to share information around issues such as climate change, biodiversity loss, and other concerns (Norton & Grecu, 2015). Giving people more information about environmental problems is a common approach to environmental communication (the information deficit disorder; Kidd et al., 2019). However, there is a growing awareness that the fundamental challenge activists face in addressing environmental problems is not increasing knowledge, but rather bridging the gap between information and action in order to change human behaviour (Jacobson et al., 2015).

A better understanding of the principles of effective collective action will help environmental activists to design campaign materials to prompt responses, which we would propose should be related to particular ABIASCA tasks. There are increasing efforts demonstrating the effects of particular messaging framing on message receivers (e.g., see Nisbet, 2009; also Newman, Nisbet, & Nisbet, 2018, on selective processing of climate change messages). This includes research on what message characteristics may be more likely to prompt specific behavioural responses (e.g., generating sympathy versus intentions versus actual action). We hope that this evidence base continues to grow, as the science of environmental communication develops further.

et al., 2013). Advocates who care about the group and identify with it are important both in internal contests among factions to choose particular tactics, and in swaying the broader bystander community. Demonstrating commitment to a shared, common group that unites bystanders with activists and their constituencies, and demonstrating a commitment to support the other norms of the group, provide powerful levers for 'identity entrepreneurship' and influence over others.

An interesting point emerging from this literature is that there is an important fork in the road – or so it seems to us – about whether activists choose to appeal to bystanders as outsiders who should live up to their own (bystander) groups' ideals and interests, or choose to appeal to bystanders to 'stand with' the activists and their constituencies as part of a shared common group (Saab, Tausch, Spears, & Cheung, 2015; Subašić, Reynolds, & Turner, 2008). Louis and colleagues (2019) suggested that the label 'solidarity' could be used to describe the collective action occurring when bystanders are led to see themselves as part of a shared, common group with the co-acting beneficiaries of their action (e.g., Hoskin, Thomas, & McGarty, 2019; Louis et al., 2019; Thomas, McGarty, Stuart, Smith, & Bourgeois, 2019). For example, when people identify with citizens of another country as fellow human beings, they may be motivated to provide for their welfare, and to support their rights and freedoms. In contrast, other people might be motivated to support foreigners' welfare because it is linked to the national interests of the helpers – for example, by preventing future migration crises. Louis and colleagues (2019) suggest that when groups are helping outsiders in order to serve their own groups' interests, this could be called allyship. One hypothesis that awaits empirical testing is whether motives of solidarity, as opposed to allyship, might increase activists' willingness to empower the targets of aid, to accept them as equals, and to avoid toxic power struggles and attempts to co-opt the movement for tangential other goals.

4.4 Frames That Are Unlikely to Work

An approach highlighting common identity and seeking to build solidarity may be contrasted with three other activist approaches which (we would argue) have little empirical justification in the present scholarly literature. One frame that seems unlikely to be effective is to communicate messages highlighting that the actors feel ashamed of a group membership shared with the bystanders (e.g., Jacquet, 2017). For example, it is common for activists seeking national reform to speak of being ashamed of their country, or activists for reform of a political party to reference being ashamed of their party. There is little evidence basis for this approach, to our knowledge, in persuading new audiences of the need for change. On the basis of past research, a message seeking to shame the audience will (all other things being equal) cause the bystander to stigmatise the messenger and reject their message (e.g., Hornsey, Trembath, & Gunthorpe, 2004).

A second potentially ineffective tactic is to highlight the hypocrisy or inconsistency of the broader public in contrast to the activists, whose moral worth is implicitly positioned as superior. This message is problematic on two levels: it distances the messengers (i.e., activists) from the target and invites the outsider label, reducing the common identity that could effectively mobilise. However, there is a second concern: this frame also identifies a contradiction between what people in a group are actually doing (sometimes called the descriptive or behavioural norm), and what people in a group think should be done (sometimes called the injunctive norm; Schultz, Nolan, Cialdini, Goldstein, & Griskevicius, 2007).

Unfortunately, there is little evidence that highlighting widespread hypocrisy motivates a group to change. Instead, there is evidence that doing so can legitimise the hypocrisy as acceptable (McKimmie et al., 2003). Stressing that a behaviour is morally wrong but common can even produce a backlash that increases the problem behaviour and decreases the target behaviour (Smith & Louis, 2008; 2009). Experiments have shown (e.g., for pro-environmental behaviour, Smith et al., 2012) that making salient a contradiction between what people do and think should be done has the effect of not just failing to shift the action, but even of significantly lowering intentions to act – that is, producing a backlash or backfire effect.

The instinct of campaign designers is often that such a message will serve as a call to arms. In Smith and Louis (2008), and in McDonald, Fielding, and Louis (2014), the research suggested that drawing attention to norm conflict functioned as a call to arms for some people: those who already considered the issue to be more personally involving or important, or who already rejected the problem behaviour and supported the target behaviour more strongly. Yet these are rarely the target of activists' campaigns or messages. For people who are more oppositional or lukewarm, according to the research mentioned, messages of norm conflict served to demobilise them. So in using this frame in their communication, activists may be preaching to the converted, using messages that motivate themselves and demotivate others.

A third ineffective tactic, we would argue from the literature, is to present differences of opinion and condemnation from other groups, such as family, workplace, organisation, nation, and others – as if they would spur changes in the target. We would argue that unless the target already agrees with the message and identifies with the group(s) providing the criticism, highlighting contradictions among the relevant normative messages is likely to lower support for the message (McDonald, Fielding, & Louis, 2013; McDonald et al., 2014). Research has shown that messengers from outgroups are typically ignored altogether (Terry et al., 1999). But such messages also may make salient bystander's own group memberships, heightening the likelihood of complying with one's own group's norms. In many circumstances, then, such an intervention could polarise bystanders away from the target group and entrench the problem action.

The challenges of identifying frames that effectively mobilise bystanders – as well as of identifying effective frames for supporters and how they may differ from those for bystanders – invite scholars' urgent research attention. A growing body of research (e.g., Feinberg, Willer, & Kovacheff, 2020; Simpson, Willer, & Feinberg, 2018) cautions that activists' intuitions may not always align with the most effective frames. In this context, identifying what works would have important benefits for activists' collective efforts, as well as in clarifying rival theories (Louis, 2009; Louis et al., 2020).

5 Opponents

In this section, we review the conditions for opponents' social influence, particularly demobilisation (persuading opponents to stand down from their opposition) and radicalisation. We conceptualise opponents in this section as those who are not merely indifferent to the cause being promoted or change being advocated for, but who would actively prefer to see the activists defeated, and may even be campaigning to block the activists' influence.

To some, it may seem counter-intuitive to think of opponents as a target or audience for action; activists on one side or the other of an issue may both more naturally orient to bystanders, supporters, and third parties such as the media, seeking to capture their attention and to sway and mobilise them. In this approach, opponents are rivals who can be defeated but are never engaged: they are competitors in the same tasks (building sympathy, intentions, etc.) with zero-sum outcomes – we will win and they will lose, or vice versa. Certainly, there is considerable evidence that opponents are disproportionately difficult to persuade, and easy to trigger into counter-mobilisation. In this sense, it is much more effective and appropriate for activists to keep a resolute focus on sympathisers (Section 3), bystanders (Section 4), and third parties (Section 6), who may be more receptive to activists' messages and actions, and less likely to be alienated by them.

However, we also examine in the present section evidence that opponents are sometimes defined too broadly by activists. We argue that there is an evidence basis validating the strategy of defining the opponents narrowly, and seeking to exploit divisions within the opponents' groups. Activists may also seek to influence opponents' constituents by drawing these constituents into broader, inclusive categories for which a leadership and norm contest is being waged. Such an approach faces the challenge of avoiding opponents' radicalisation, and (as we cover in Section 6) the dynamics of mutual radicalisation that can affect both supporters and opponents in political contests. However, it is possible that an actor who is an opponent now will capitulate to a demand, or transform into a supporter, building collective efficacy claims and cementing a much stronger coalition and message frame around the issue. Taking this approach, opponents can be conceptualised as allies in waiting.

5.1 In General, Opponents Dismiss Activists' Outreach and Backlash

Let us begin by restating that if activists reach out to opponents with some sort of change message, these messages and messengers are often ignored altogether (Fielding, Hornsey, Thai, & Toh, 2019; Terry et al., 1999). As we highlighted in Section 4, a message about what other groups do which is different and superior to what our group does is likely to make salient one's own group memberships. When a group membership is made salient, group members tend to perceive greater similarities within their own group and differences from other groups (Turner et al., 1987). The greater salience of one's in-group identity will increase the likelihood of dismissing messages from other groups. Such group dynamics ensure that we do not change our views and actions when we come into contact with outsiders – otherwise, we could change our religion every time we met someone from a new congregation, and our politics with every different conversation that we engage in, at work or in an airport.

Yet the difficulty of influencing opponents does not just arise from the likelihood that they will ignore and dismiss outsiders' influence attempts: there are also processes of backlash and polarisation (Louis et al., 2018; Louis et al., 2020). An outcome of outsiders' persuasion attempts is that it will lead to greater rejection of their attitudes and actions, and increased affirmation of one's own group's norms and values. One reason is identity-based: when opponents' identities become more salient (allowing rejection of outsider influence), it simultaneously increases their likelihood of affirming and enacting their own groups' norms. If an outsider says 'believe in my God' or 'vote for my party', the response may not be simply to remain unmoved, but rather to feel a stronger belief in one's own religious or political convictions. Outsiders' influence attempts may also be perceived as explicitly offensive or threatening, generating a response that reflects that threat. The net result may be both increased conviction regarding one's own beliefs, values, and actions paired with a stronger rejection of the others' beliefs, values, and actions.

Indeed, as we saw in Table 1 of Section 2, activists' orientation to opponents is not always just to try to persuade them to join the actors' cause. Collective action oriented to opponents may come with communication of explicit hostility from the activists to opponents: rejection of their values; violation of their norms; and perhaps even an expressed desire to harm, defeat, or destroy opponents as a group. Such out-group hostility or norm violations are very strong predictors of identity salience and identification for the opponents who are targeted, and unsurprisingly they are also triggers for opponents' collective action and counter-mobilisation (e.g., Hayward, Tropp, Hornsey, & Barlow,

2018; Louis, Taylor, & Douglas, 2005; Louis et al., 2020). For most activists, counter-mobilising opponents is to be avoided in and of itself (Louis et al., 2010). Expressing hostility and contempt towards opponents also may trigger opponent radicalisation, as we shall now see.

5.2 Activists May Cause Opponents to Radicalise

Research on radicalisation might seem to sit more naturally in Section 3 (on mobilising supporters) than in this section. Indeed, some empirical research links social interaction among supporters in the form of active debate, negotiation, and discussion, with collective mobilisation (Bongiorno, McGarty, Kurz, Haslam, & Sibley, 2016; Thomas, McGarty, & Mavor, 2009; Thomas et al., 2016; Thomas et al., 2019) and, under the right circumstances, shifts towards extremism (Smith, Blackwood, & Thomas, 2020; Thomas, McGarty, & Louis, 2014). However, we do not consider that radicalisation is a natural part of supporter mobilisation dynamics. Our approach is that it is typically a product of the intergroup relationship with opponents (Drury & Reicher, 2009; Louis et al., 2020), and thus we focus on the processes of radicalisation within this opponent section. Box 6 discusses the recent dynamics of Black Lives Matter and Alt-Right movements, as one contemporary example of opponent radicalisation.

According to the model of radicalisation put forward by Kruglanski and colleagues (Kruglanski, Bélanger, & Gunaratna, 2019; Webber & Kruglanski, 2018; Webber et al., 2017), violent extremism emerges when a *need* for personal significance combines with a *narrative* that ideologically justifies violence and spreads through a *network* of others who make it normatively acceptable and expected. The same model may be applied in deradicalisation, to imagine how peace and compromise spread within a violent network. So how can scholars understand – and activists perhaps intervene – in the radicalising narratives of opponents?

While we have earlier in Section 4 used the term 'frame', we can unpack the idea of 'narrative' in radicalisation research as drawing attention to the same elements of diagnosis of a problem, proposal of a solution, and formation of an invitation or a norm to act. One point that is important for our purposes is that when the problem diagnosis includes the perceived threats or intransigence of one's opponents, and the solution frame includes the perceived ineffectiveness of conventional tactics, these are often core elements of narratives of support for activists' radicalisation. Therefore, when opponents communicate intransigence and imperviousness to conventional tactics, it is a spur to some activists' support for radical actions (e.g., Blackwood & Louis, 2017; Louis et al., 2020), particularly when moral language is used (Mooijman, Hoover, Lin, Ji, &

An important component of the Black Lives Matter movement is its opposition to police brutality and state-sanctioned violence (Giddings, 2009). BLM activists organise protests to draw attention to police violence and other racial disparities around economic, social, and political power. Indeed, police-related civilian deaths increase the likelihood of BLM protests in an area (Williamson, Trump, & Einstein, 2018). Yet despite the many unnecessary and unjust deaths that have been documented, not all communities and authorities have welcomed the invitation to reform. Responses from state actors have included both legal and extra-legal tactics to obstruct the protests, including criminalisation and surveillance (see also Lopez, 2001). Another community response has been a growth in the 'alt-right' movement. While alt-right activists are diverse in their attempts to cultivate grassroots support for various agendas, some are attempting to normalise white nationalist discourse and even white supremacy (Nagle, 2017). The dynamic growth of BLM and alt-right groups has also resulted in violent confrontations between anti-racist and white nationalist protesters. In this sense, both state and community actors have shown opponent radicalisation in the face of the BLM protests.

Opponent radicalisation in turn may affect some activists' own radic-alisation trajectories, with implications for bystander evaluations and supporter mobilisation. One recent study shows that when instigated by anti-racist protesters, BLM violence was found to decrease support for the anti-racist group; in contrast, support for white nationalists was not reduced when BLM activists instigated violence (Simpson, Willer, & Feinberg, 2018). Other research has found that groups engaging in violent tactics do lose public support, however (Feinberg, Willer, & Kovacheff, 2020; Thomas & Louis, 2014; see also Ellefsen, 2018). This is an area that warrants future investigation.

Dehghani, 2018). In turn, when opponents communicate that they will not be moved by radical tactics, and they are open to conventional tactics, these may be prompts to activists' support for conventional actions. Thus each side's stated tactical preferences or openness to change have the potential to inform oppon-ents' choices (Lizzio-Wilson et al., 2021; Louis et al., 2020). Box 7 discusses such a dynamic in the context of relations between Right-Wing and Islamist Violent Extremism in Europe.

Approaching the topic from another angle: it is the content of activists' discus-sions that determines whether violence and lawbreaking are given moral approval,

Box 7 Opponent Radicalisation in Europe: Muslim Jihadists and Extreme Nationalists

The tension in the twenty-first century between Muslims and non-Muslims in Europe has at times broken out into violence committed by Islamists or right-wing extremists (Moghaddam, 2018). In European non-Muslim communities, as well as within Muslim communities, many citizens continue to support democracy, human rights, and multicultural Europe. However, membership in groups of right-wing extremists and Muslim violent jihadists has also grown, in some communities, as some opponents are radicalised by the actions of the other.

Some non-Muslim Europeans may feel threatened by the growth of a Muslim European community perceived to have different values and norms, or some Muslims may feel threatened when secular values are asserted as core to European governance (Simon & Grabow, 2010). Yet more concretely, mass murders and terrorist acts by extremists on one side serve to prompt and legitimise contempt, hatred, and retaliation from extremists on the other side (Louis et al., 2020; Moghaddam, 2018). Attempts to counter the radicalisation of the other occur therefore not only through civil political debates on the future of European society, but in some communities, in the form of mutually growing prejudice, and willingness to entertain lawbreaking and violence. Interrupting this cycle of opponent radicalisation is a central concern not only of scholars, but of authorities more broadly (Louis et al., 2020; Moghaddam, 2016; Moghaddam, 2016; 2018).

seen as a regrettable necessity, judged to be permissible but ineffective, or rejected as immoral and proscribed (Thomas et al., 2014; Smith et al., 2020). If we return to the DIME model presented in Section 2, and theorise that opponents' effective action may be seen as a failure prompt for activists' groups, we would expect on the basis of DIME that every 'effective' activist collective action risks energising and radicalising at least a minority of opponents. In some cases, this may in fact be desirable in the eyes of some activists: radicalising some opponents may benefit an activist movement, to the extent that the actions of the radical factions or wings of the opponents' movement then alienate bystanders and reduce third parties' support (Feinberg, Willer & Kovacheff, 2020; Simpson, Willer & Feinberg, 2018; Thomas & Louis, 2014). In other cases, radicalising opponents may mean a greater danger of conflict escalation, polarisation, reduced social cohesion, and stalemates, and thus much less chance that activists can effectively achieve their goals (Louis et al., 2018; 2020). While we acknowledge that there are complexities that are not being elaborated in the Element – a comprehensive exploration of the pros and cons of radicalisation must be left to another Element – if we assume that activists sometimes desire to engage opponents without radicalising them, is there an evidence basis for how to proceed?

5.3 Divide and Conquer? How Activists Can Exploit Opponents' Factionalism

A strategy with a higher probability of success may be one that involves fracturing or dividing one's opponents, in line with the old adage of 'divide and conquer'. There are three aspects of this strategy that are important from a social psychological perspective: opponents' factionalism, overlapping group memberships, and shared (superordinate) groups. We shall address each in turn.

It is a truism to say that group unity is idealised and ephemeral, while day-to-day life is riven with factions, disputes, schisms, and debates (Louis, Chonu, Achia, Chapman, & Rhee, 2018; McCarthy & Zald, 1977; Sani & Reicher, 1998; Sani & Reicher, 2000). Factional conflict between groups of activists proposing different tactics can affect responses to campaigns and movement effectiveness, as we have just seen; it can also give rise to competition for donations and activists. Partisan or factional conflict can even assume a dominant role such that effectiveness becomes defined in terms of defeating opponents for control of the movement, rather than actually achieving the movement's original goals.

In addressing this point, Louis and colleagues (2018) theorised that political groups exist in an ongoing ferment of new, erupting subgroups or factions, created by differentiation pressures. Even where a consensus is presented at a higher superordinate level, there are sometimes divergent subgroups at a lower level: regions within nations; factions within political parties; denominations within faiths, and so on. These may be invisible from the outside, as if the group presents a consensus, or a smooth bell curve of variability. But from the inside the group's norms appear 'lumpy': there are distinct subgroups with different points of view, and there are emerging or emergent challenges to the broader group's views and actions (see also Pareto, 1935; Moghaddam, 2013, 2016).

For the purposes of the present Element, the point is that these factions' political conflict and the constraints of the political environment together create oscillations over time: the larger group or polity repetitively cycles between the different normative positions that are held by its factions (Louis et al., 2018). This oscillation of power from faction to faction within a society is actually an explicit aim of democratic systems. However, even outside democracies, changes of power from clique to clique of an autocracy, or family to family of an oligarchy, also occur due to competing factional desires to take power and to address constituents' concerns and to reward them materially. As these factions' concerns are met and they benefit, other factions grow hungrier, make more alliances, and more urgently seek to take control. Louis et al. (2018) proposed that these oscillations are an empirical reality that invite scholars' attention, and that they are associated with broader shifts in political and social norms.

We propose in the present Element that consideration of opponents' factionalism, and of the probability of internal leadership contests and change over time, is relevant to activists' goals of opponent influence. Within each electoral cycle or leadership contest, the issues and frames that groups use to contest the event change. Each side seeks to frame their pitch in terms of including a winning coalition of interests, and opposing a minority's views. Before, during, and after the intergroup contests of supporters and opponents, there are internal factional contests to control the leadership and direction of the movements, parties, or groups. Thus even if present-day opponents are rigidly refusing a desired change, future opponent leaders might be led to establish a consensus, or to make concessions on activists' target issues. One direction of collective action aimed at opponents is therefore to invite a faction of the opponents to unite with some or all of the activists, to create what will become a majority viewpoint on a particular direction of policy change. This strategy of formal or informal coalition building means that if either the activists *or* the opponent faction of the other party or group take power, the policy change can occur.

A coalition like this across divides such as party lines is strongly deterred and policed by the leadership on either side, for obvious reasons. It may be seen as treacherous, or accurately identified as threatening to those who seek polarisation or to promote extremist stances. As a result, an effective collective action aimed at opponents often rests on two important identity dynamics: those of cross-cutting or overlapping group memberships, and those of shared or superordinate groups.

The concept of cross-cutting group memberships refers to the fact that although activists may be divided from opponents by their stand on a particular issue, they may be united with (some of) them by other group memberships, in demographic categories such as gender, region, religion, or ethnicity, as well as with particular opinion group identities (Bliuc, McGarty, Reynolds, & Muntele, 2007; McGarty et al., 2009; Smith, Thomas, & McGarty, 2015). An opinion group identity is an identity defined by a stand on a particular issue – for example, as pro-life versus pro-choice (Ntontis & Hopkins, 2018), or as 'Remain' versus 'Leave' in the Brexit debate (Hobolt, Leeper, & Tilley, 2020). Such identities may be held lightly or passionately, and like other identities, some are not very important in everyday life – but they are often a relatively strong predictor of collective action (Bliuc et al., 2015; Thomas et al., 2012). Opinion-based identities are often clustered within higher order ideological identities and party identities, but they also cross party lines and may form and dissolve more fluidly (Louis et al., 2020). When a new opinion group identity forms, or becomes newly linked to activist action, such as #MeToo or the 99%, this can trigger a new wave of collective action (Simon & Klandermans, 2001).

For the purpose of the present section, the key point is that an effective collective action aimed at opponents is often one that redefines the issue as being about a cross-cutting identity, rather than an ideological identity, or even the primary opinion group identity. Ideological or opinion group identities may lead activists to be divided from opponents and thus invoking them is unlikely to be persuasive. A pro-life advocate may polarise a pro-choice audience, and vice versa. However, if the issue can be linked to some other cross-cutting identity on which (some of) the opponents may legitimately be mobilised in coalition with (some of) the activists, the activists can join with a subset of their opponents and move towards a coalition or bipartisan consensus view (see also Ben David & Rubel-Lifschitz, 2018).

The impact of polarised identities has been demonstrated empirically. For example, Unsworth & Fielding (2014) found in two experimental studies that raising the salience of an individual's political identity resulted in lower support for climate change policies in individuals with right-wing beliefs. There are methods to overcome this effect, however. By holding a ceremony, giving an award, or forming a panel that presents a cross-cutting identity-based coalition, organisers may successfully establish that some others – industry or regional subgroups, or ethnic or religious minorities, or women or men, or sexual minorities, or any other cross-cutting identity – also have a stand on this issue compatible with that of activists. Accordingly, the stage is set for these factions within the opponent group to become publicly visible, and to have internal influence in becoming champions within their group for the activists' advocacy position. While some theorising addresses this possibility (Louis et al., 2020), there is little research that directly speaks to the operation of these tactics, and therefore it would be a valuable direction of future research to demonstrate these coalition-building processes to divide opponent groups within controlled, experimental settings.

5.4 Activists Can Assert a Shared Identity That Includes Opponents

An alternative approach to opponent influence is simply to seek to assimilate the constituency of the opponents within one's own, by affirming a shared or superordinate identity that encompasses both groups, and which the activists define and frame in line with their own values and priorities. For example, shared nation and/or faith is often rhetorically deployed by activists as underpinning their minority point of view. An effective example of this positioning is provided by Martin Luther King's 'I have a dream' speech, which powerfully located egalitarian and anti-racist values within a broader American identity. In the current world context, it is striking that any given national identity is often simultaneously being linked to racist or anti-immigrant mobilisation by some activists, through exclusionary representations and symbols of (ethnically defined) heritage, and at the same time also linked to anti-racist mobilisation by others, through inclusive representations (e.g., see Berndsen, Thomas, & Pedersen, 2018; Doucerain et al., 2018). Similarly, authorities and opponents frequently identify collective action itself as inconsistent with national or religious identities, in order to attempt to limit support for the movement and demobilise supporters (Andits, 2016). Thus contesting what it means to be part of a broader (superordinate) group identity is a common task and element of effective collective action frames.

An approach of speaking benevolently from presumed shared interests and values invites activists to communicate warmth and inclusion towards opponents. This is a strategy that might be seen as taking the moral high ground, or as a form of identity entrepreneurship (Reicher, Hopkins, Levine, & Rath, 2005; Steffens et al., 2013), or as 'love bombing' (Robbins, 1984) intentionally designed to elicit change. Such an influence strategy is perhaps more effective when the conflict is novel, and not too extreme or protracted, or linked to other social and ideological fissures. But even in those intractable conflicts, communicating warmth, openness, and respect may be able to have an impact when other conditions are met (Bar-Tal, 2000).

At the individual and interpersonal levels, a warm and inclusive approach to opponents might focus on creating positive interpersonal contact, and taking the opportunity to affirm similar values and establish common fate. These strategies have been specifically found to erode opponent militancy by reducing the salience of the opponent identity (e.g., Greenaway, Quinn, & Louis, 2011; Reimer et al., 2017). Communicating that it is possible to move between opinion groups could also reduce collective action intentions by reducing the salience of identity (Tausch, Saguy, & Bryson, 2015), although to our knowledge this has not been experimentally demonstrated in relation to opinion group mobilisation. A final (nefarious) strategy is tokenism, by which we mean intentionally including visible but unrepresentative opponents within the advantaged minority of a broad superordinate group, as a way to promote constituents' superordinate identification and reduce mobilisation

(Danaher & Branscombe, 2010; Wright & Taylor, 1998; see also Platow et al., 2013). These strategies have demotivated opponents in experimental research, although again to our knowledge they have not been tested in opinion group field contexts.

5.5 When Can Activists Deradicalise Opponent Groups?

As a last point within the section on opponent influence, we will consider the challenge of deradicalising opponent groups. In the literature on deradicalisation (e.g., Horgan, 2008; Horgan, Altier, Shortland, & Taylor, 2017; Marsden, 2016), scholars and practitioners have distinguished desistance (in which individual opponents stop engaging in the action – for example, because they are imprisoned), disengagement (in which group members leave a radical opponent group), and ideological deradicalisation (in which opponent group members abandon their commitment to the social change ideologies that the radical group advocates). Some scholars highlight common pathways across these deradicalisation outcomes, so that the same factors that promote radicalisation are involved in deradicalisation (Webber & Kruglanski, 2018; Webber et al., 2017). However, from a group process perspective, these different trajectories would not be expected to be mutually reinforcing.

Interventions that encourage, for example, the individual members of a group who are least committed to radical actions, or most interested in conventional tactics, to simply desist from the radical actions or to drop out of the group, have the potential to reduce the likelihood that the group will change its norms as a whole (Louis et al., 2020). Instead, the departure of more 'moderate' activists will leave the group intact and purified in its commitment to radicalism. Thus desistance and disengagement will only work to deradicalise a group if they have the capacity to reduce the number of group members to below the membership required to keep functioning. This could only occur in the event that no other recruits are available to replace the exiting moderate or demotivated members.

It is even possible that such interventions designed to foster disengagement, desistance, or ideological deradicalisation may slow the pace of change by undermining the moral authority of advocates for conventional forms of action within a group. Norm change to shift from radical tactics to more conventional tactics is not uncommon: transitioning to rejoin the political process is a common exit path from terror, and more broadly radical groups also frequently return to the fold of conventional actions (e.g., Jones & Libicki, 2008). Before and after the transition of a group from radical to more conventional tactics, there will be an internal norm contest where group members and factional leaders may debate which tactics are more effective and in line with the group's goals and values. In this context, the potential of disengagement strategies to undermine long-term deradicalisation becomes clear. In one study of violent groups in Northern Ireland, the presence of former violent combatants as leaders of the pro-peace transition was found to be critical in bringing about the group's norm change towards peace (Ferguson, McDaid, & McAuley, 2018; see also Flack & Ferguson, in press). Having faced combat and imprisonment, while remaining committed to the group's ideological goals, was important in credentialing the leaders' persuasive efforts to shift the group's tactics towards peace. In contrast, if moderate views become associated with desertion or lack of commitment to the group, the influence of moderate norms is far less likely to prevail.

Taking a step back, from the theoretical perspective of Social Identity Theory, changing opponents' norms towards deradicalisation rests on changing perceptions of the intergroup relationship between the groups in the contest. Specifically, opponents must come to believe that the relationship between the groups is more stable, more permeable, and/or more legitimate. In-group leaders are always going to be more effectively persuasive, for the reasons described at length in Section 3 and Section 4. However, out-group leaders can seek to signal the legitimacy of the intergroup relationship by tactics such as affirming respect for opponents, giving voice to opponents, or allowing opponents into the leadership team. Affirming shared identities and respecting higher-level norms such as holding elections also may build support, and signalling cooperation with desired, conventional tactics and resistance to old, radical ones may under some circumstances allow outsiders to change perceptions of tactics' efficacy and control (Blackwood & Louis, 2017). Of course, such strategies may also be used tokenistically to undermine opponents' resolve in the short term (Platow et al., 2013; Wright & Taylor, 1998).

The bigger picture for activists is that in many conflicts, there is an internal struggle between moderates and extremists within *both* the supporter and the opponent movements. We do not by any means imply that there are not moral differences between movements, with one movement able to be judged morally as being more virtuous and the other more abominable. Rather, we are noting that intragroup conflicts between moderates and extremists on each side, can also coexist with the intergroup struggle between extremists in either camp. Thus, it is also possible to imagine that just as extremists are participating cooperatively in mutual radicalisation by communicating signals of anger, moral condemnation of the other, and escalation of aggression – with each extremist side rebroadcasting and amplifying the messages of the others' extremists – moderates within groups might seek to support mutual deradicalisation through mutual signals of respect, security, moral acceptance, and assertion of inclusive identities. There is little research to map these complex dynamics against empirical data, however.

One last point to note in this section on opponent influence is that a minority can exert influence over a majority through persuasion to the extent that it provides consistent, sacrificial advocacy (see also Subašić et al., 2008). Thus, when activists frame themselves as located within a broader community where opponents define the majority position, a strategy of seeking their own long-term minority influence can be pursued (see Section 4). Yet there is an alternative available: to appeal to third parties, such as the media and decision makers, over the heads of opponents. This is a strategy that we will take up in the next section.

6 Third Parties

In this section we focus specifically on effective collective action directed at other interest groups, which we here refer to as 'third parties'. The present Element addresses three specific third-party categories: activists for other causes, the media, and policy makers. These groups are chosen as effective collective action often involves forming alliances, obtaining supportive media coverage, and influencing political outcomes. In order to gain third-party support, as we shall see, activists must sustain and mobilise their group while pre-empting counter-mobilisation from other groups. What conditions assist groups in achieving this goal? And what conditions facilitate failure?

The backdrop for this section is the contention that it is not only by converting bystanders and opponents to supporters that a movement 'wins' the desired social and policy changes. Rather, success can be influenced by convincing powerful others to support the activists' cause for their own purposes. As such, activists and their groups are influenced by their own past decisions, expectations, norms, and identities, but also by a broader social context in which they must build alliances or coalitions with other parties and disrupt their opponents' coalitions (Ayanian & Tausch, 2016; Bliuc, McGarty, Hartley, & Muntele, 2012; Jasper, 2019; Pareto, 1935; Subasic et al., 2008; van Zomeren & Louis, 2017).

6.1 Activism and Arenas

One way of understanding the power of the context is to use the metaphor that activists' collective action occurs within 'arenas': the social environments and physical settings where activists' interactions generate particular decisions or outcomes (Jasper, 2004; 2019). In these arenas outcomes are determined less by direct competition between groups who are supporters and opponents on a particular issue, and more by the ability of each to engage the goals and interests of other players in the arena (Duyvendak & Jasper, 2015). These other players can be individuals, groups, or 'compound players' – collections of individuals ranging from informal and loose grassroots groups to nation states – which can expand, contract, and continually redefine each other through contact with others (Fetner, 2008). How these groups interact in any given arena influences the mobilisation and tactical choices of activists, opponents' responses, and ultimately the outcomes of collective action (Meyer, 2004). Within the arenas, potential political allies, supportive public opinion, and favourable media coverage all represent opportunities which can determine the effectiveness of protest in achieving its goals (Agnone, 2007; Cress & Snow, 2000; Johnson, Agnone, & McCarthy, 2010).

As we shall shortly elaborate in greater detail, the third parties most relevant to activists' ability to engage in effective activism, we propose, are those located within the advocacy network arena, media arena, and the policy arena. The first of these is the advocacy arena. This arena includes all other activists for all other causes: identity groups such as religious or ethnic groups, as well as advocacy organisations pursuing goals and interests unrelated to those of the focal activists. They are relevant to activists' effectiveness because these groups may become allies or opponents of the activists. Activist groups seek to gain support from others in order to create a 'chain of trust' (Louis et al., 2020) to power holders, and to build strong and sustained coalitions pooling resources to pursue shared goals (e.g., Heumann & Duyvendak, 2015; Tarrow, 2011). As mentioned in Section 4 on bystanders, and as we will cover in depth here, both formal and informal coalitions may emerge from points of normative consistency among groups, or cross-cutting identities (e.g., geographic regions). These coalitions can draw on shared identities or common values to create networks of trusted communication links that allow for loosely coordinated action and mutual support, as seen for example, in support for climate change action by labour unions and medical groups.

The media arena has also been a focus of research on the outcomes of collective action, as mentioned in our discussion of bystanders. Both traditional and social media channels help to disseminate and frame social change messages, and therefore shape the public agenda, influencing public opinion, and through that encouraging politicians to act in accordance with public wishes (Andrews & Caren, 2010; Burstein, 2003). As a result, activists seek media support and favourable coverage as an important strategy for building public support and mobilisation for their cause. The media arena includes as players publishers, broadcasters, and powerful media conglomerates, but can also include groups such as experts and intellectuals. For example, scientists in the media arena may be active both in reinforcing power holders' messages and sometimes in undermining them (Cordner, Brown, & Mulcahy, 2015).

The final arena that we highlight is the policy arena, where many activist campaigns directly seek to elicit policy change and/or target political entities (e.g., Gulliver, Fielding, & Louis, 2019). Actors in this arena include activists as well as policy makers, government departments, lobby groups, think tanks, and corporations, all of whom both act and are acted upon by others in the arena (Dobbin & Jung, 2015).

6.2 The Importance of Coalition Building

In the following sections we consider four factors that can influence whether activists gain third-party support: coalition building, activists' tactical repertoires, counter-mobilisation and the radicalisation of state actors, and state repression. The central point is that in each different arena, coalitions are important for the long-term survival of activists' groups as well as for their ability to achieve their collective goals (Edwards & McCarthy, 2004; McCarthy & Zald, 1977; van Dyke & Amos, 2017). As shown by the example in Box 8, coalition building may enable greater exploitation of windows of opportunities. For example, circumstances such as a decline in repression, division within the political arena, or increased organisational resources could enhance activists' ability to achieve their aims and drive major policy change (McAdam, 1982; Tarrow, 2011). Coalitions and strategic alliances may shift considerably over time: major policy change may be driven by coalitions effectively exploiting disruptive events such as the release of new evidence demonstrating bureaucratic deficiencies, natural disasters, and other government crises (Sotirov & Winkel, 2016). However, these strategies are not always sufficient for driving major policy change alone, as other powerful coalitions of opponents may block successful changes. Coalitions can also shrink and dissolve over time, because groups within the social movement community or ecosystem are in a constant flux of competition or cooperation (e.g., Staggenborg, 1998). Engagement in one activist group may inhibit engagement in others, and activists (and factions) can disengage from movements when other causes emerge which better serve their motives and resources, or which seem to offer greater opportunities (Edwards et al., 2018).

The intergroup dynamics enabling such shifts in coalitions' support to occur can be understood using the Advocacy Coalition Framework (ACF; Jenkins-Smith, 1990; Sabatier, 1998; Sabatier & Jenkins-Smith, 1993). The ACF considers how people mobilise and act in advocacy coalitions to influence policy change (Sotirov & Winkel, 2016). Individuals are proposed to seek out like-

The Stop the Bioterror Lab Coalition was a coalition between environmental justice activists and the peace and anti-weapons-proliferation movement in the United States (Beamish & Luebbers, 2009). Seeking to stop the building of a biocontainment laboratory, the coalition was notable due to its successes in building a coalition which crossed groups with different causes and grievances. Beamish and Luebbers (2009) identified how this cross-identity coalition formed and was sustained until the outcome was effectively achieved, most importantly by affirming the central cause of the alliance while also linking to a range of other social grievances.

Through the campaigns, the proposed lab became a symbol of how the local community was marginalised, as well as overlooked in political decision-making around development proposals (Beamish & Luebbers, 2009). This linkage broadened the campaign goal to include many more activists, while offering a greater range of solutions beyond winning the focal campaign itself (i.e., to block the lab). Through adopting a broader frame, the activists turned third-party characteristics argued to hinder coalition building, such as divergent identities and ideologies, into assets. Accordingly, the alliance not only achieved its stated goal of stopping the lab development, but also persisted as a vehicle for social change after its initial victory condition was met.

minded allies – including state, private sector, civil society, and media – to form coalitions which can influence policy outcomes over long periods of time (Weible & Sabatier, 2007). For our purposes, the key points to stress in applying the ACF to the concept of effective activism are that most policy arenas have multiple competing interest coalitions, with different problem definitions and solutions, and different advocacy frames (Boscarino, 2016). These competing advocacy coalitions seek to broaden problem definitions and solutions to attract support from other groups who may be focused on related issues (Dodge, 2016).

Despite the complexity of the intergroup dynamics, a generalisation is that arenas are prone to states of gridlock or rigidity under pressure. For example, Dodge (2016) found that the dynamics of 'crowded advocacy' in the hydraulic fracking debate in New York between 2007 and 2014 created intense mobilisation and counter-mobilisation that resulted in policy controversies becoming polarised and intractable. Lejano and Dodge (2017) identified the same dynamic for American climate change activism more broadly. Polarised, gridlocked states occur when dominant coalitions become entrenched in their particular policy positions during policy conflicts. They change when third parties are influenced by reframing of issues (see Section 4 on framing), and when coalitions therefore shift and open space for policy resolution.

One line of work on effective coalition building stresses that groups will be more likely to be effective in recruiting coalition partners when their shared properties, functions, and relations are better aligned with group members' psychological states (e.g., see Dixon & Levine, 2012; Spears, 2010). Social psychological research (as we have seen in earlier sections) also highlights the importance of shared identity in determining responses of third parties to activists' demands. For example, the Social Identities in the Political Process model (SIPP: Hornung, Bandelow, & Vogeler, 2019) proposes that collective identities shape group members' views on policy content, and create the desire to benefit the newly forming coalition. Similarly, van Dyke and Amos (2017) highlight identity as one of the five factors influencing effective coalition formation (the others being social ties, conducive organisational structures, institutional environment, and resources).

These models converge on the proposal that by affirming shared identities and relationships with other advocacy groups, activists build stronger network ties, which then can increase the potential for a group to achieve its goals (see also Edwards & McCarthy, 2004; McCarthy & Zald, 1977). When social identities overlap, the shared normative content (e.g., shared beliefs, emotions, actions, and values) may make coalition forming more likely. Coalition building may therefore be more likely to succeed when activists highlight shared or intersectional identities (Curtin & McGarty, 2016; Louis et al., 2020; Subasic, Reynolds, & Turner, 2008; Tarrow & Tilly, 2007). Similarities in shared emotional responses, particularly for aversive events generating strong negative emotions, have also been shown to be powerful in creating new shared identities (Whitehouse et al., 2014, 2017). These new shared identities can then provide the vehicle to pull individuals and groups into activists' coalitions.

6.3 The Influence of Activists' Tactical Repertoires

Activists' tactical repertoires also affect the likelihood of successfully engaging third parties in the various arenas. One aspect is that the challenge of creating frames which attract sympathy is made more complex by the need to gain the attention of other actors, especially the attention of the media. Attracting media attention requires a constant reinvention of new styles of protest and imagery to create novelty that lures journalists' fluctuating interests (Lester & Hutchins, 2009, 2012). More novel issues or confrontational tactics, for example, generate more local media attention than routine advocacy tactics undertaken by professional groups on established issues (e.g., Andrews & Caren, 2010). Thus, many researchers have highlighted how activists use disruptive tactics to gain coverage and elevate their issue in the public arenas (Lester & Hutchins, 2009; Mazumder, 2018).

In some cases even hostile media coverage may provide awareness-raising benefits that activists can exploit in attempts to gain sympathy. For example, scholars have shown that the media has played an important role in disseminating far right messages, and one reason is that radical right activists' messages are often framed around conflict and hence are more 'newsworthy' (Aalberg, Esser, Reinemann, Stromback, & De Vreese, 2016). Electoral analyses show that the dissemination of far right messages by populist decision makers and the media has lifted support for the movement (Mazzoleni, 2003). Yet in other cases awareness may not translate to sympathy.

In one analysis, Wasow (2020) described the capturing of media and political attention as 'agenda seeding'. Using non-violent US civil rights collective action as the basis for his analysis, Wasow demonstrated how non-violent action that was met with state or vigilante repression led to increased media coverage as well as congressional speeches, and more supportive public opinion measures on civil rights. On the other hand, protesters who initiated violent collective action produced negative responses on those same measures. Indeed, other recent research we have already noted indicates that 'extreme' protest tactics – disruptive actions or those that are harmful to others – can reduce bystanders' identification with the movement (Feinberg, Willer, & Kovacheff, 2020; Simpson, Willer, & Feinberg, 2018). The ability to retain a strong moral compass is one of the factors identified by Ben David and Rubel-Lifschitz (2018) as characterising activist groups in their case studies who achieved success (the other two factors being rejecting simple binaries, and initiating small symbolic acts, timed and leveraged to build trust and attract reciprocation). Of course, ensuring tactics remain non-violent does not guarantee supportive media coverage.

In addition to affecting media coverage, tactical choices may also influence coalition-building outcomes. Radical tactics can demobilise and repel potential recruits. Even intentions to engage in more radical tactics have been associated with disidentification from an identity with more conventional norms (e.g., Jiménez-Moya, Spears, Rodríguez-Bailón, & de Lemus, 2015).

The ability of radical tactics to undermine cohesion may even be deliberately exploited by opponents, as we have mentioned in Section 5. Within an advocacy network, provocateur elements can sow dissent from within, seeking to elicit a choice of more militant tactics that would then have the effect of alienating others and undermining success (Chenoweth, 2020). In a less strategic manner, opponents' radical choices can also empower extremist factors towards mutual radicalisation. We have already considered this dynamic in Section 5, but we shall now consider it in more detail for the relationships between activists, opponent activists, and state actors such as the police.

6.4 Counter-Mobilisation, the Radicalisation of State Actors, and Repression

As we have highlighted in Section 5, at a psychological level the rejection of attempts by others to persuade can lead to more intense convictions about one's own norms and values. Increased social identification and moral conviction, or out-group hostility, can then trigger collective action and counter-mobilisation (Hayward et al., 2018; Louis et al., 2010, 2020). For these reasons, as we have seen, activists who are increasingly threatening, oppositional, and willing to violate opponents' or the majority's norms are likely to spur opponents to counter-mobilise and to embrace more confrontational tactics themselves (Blackwood & Louis, 2017; Livingstone, Spears, Manstead, & Bruder, 2009). When we consider the operation of these dynamics within contested arenas, scholars have argued that counter-movements are more likely to appear when three conditions are met: when movements appears to be showing signs of being effective; where vested interests are threatened by those movements; and where the counter-movement has access to political allies (e.g., Meyer & Staggenborg, 1996).

As the contest 'heats up' and both sides become more radicalised, it is common through factionalism that distinct groups of protestors, third-party groups, and subgroups of opponents form identities based on confrontational tactical preferences (Louis & Montiel, 2018; Louis et al., 2020; see also Stuart, Thomas, Donaghue, & Russell, 2013). An intergroup dynamic may emerge between tactical groups, such that each coalition's extremists justify and inflame the others, producing increasingly inflammatory language and hostility. If unchecked, such hostility may be expressed in fringe skirmishing and criminal violence (e.g., assassinations), spill over into organised gang and militia violence, as well as corporate malfeasance, or even escalate to the point of civil war (Andits, 2016; Louis et al., 2020). How can we understand such dynamics?

A first point is that where groups are interacting within a benevolent and just society, many mechanisms of dispute resolution, social norms, and learned expectancies about the rule of law will prevent factions within groups from advocating for tactics such as violence or subversion (Moghaddam, 2013, 2016). However, groups can come to use frames which delegitimise the values and norms of the rule of law and of democracy, as they struggle to acquire new allies and to understand the reluctance of policymakers to accede to their demands. At the same time, a process of mutual radicalisation may occur between protestors and state actors themselves, affecting groups such as the police, politicians, lawyers, and the judiciary. Increasingly radical activists may meet with similarly radicalised counter-movements in their opponents: increasingly authoritarian politicians, violent and brutal police, corrupt corporate entities, and pro-state vigilantes and militias (Louis et al., 2020; Moghaddam, 2018). Human rights laws may be wound back; politicians may seek to restrict and criminalise dissent; and human rights abuses may be overlooked or committed by authorities while prosecutors and judges turn a blind eye. Such dynamics further inflame activists' conviction of the illegitimacy of the state, increasing the likelihood that conflict will escalate, and that groups within an arena will be fractured through tactical debates from within.

Little empirical work speaks directly to these dynamics, however. The eruption of unplanned violence in rioting has been explored by John Drury and colleagues, whose research shows that it is when peaceful crowds encounter indiscriminate (instead of targeted) police repression of provocateur minorities that they embrace retaliatory violence and lawbreaking in return (Drury & Reicher, 2000, 2005; Drury, Stott, & Farsides, 2003; Stott, Livingstone, & Hoggett, 2008; Stott & Reicher, 2011). Other scholars have found that injustice experienced at the hands of police officers or the military creates a perception of the illegitimacy of the state, at least for some activists in the moment, which may create a rationale for lawbreaking or violence (Canetti-Nisim, Halperin, Sharvit, & Hobfoll, 2009; Canetti, Hall, Rapaport, & Wayne, 2013). In turn, scholars have shown that protestors' lawbreaking and violence is seen by some police and military personnel as a legitimate trigger for state violence, aimed at protecting the public and public order (Drury et al., 2003; Monaghan & Walby, 2012; Soares, Barbosa, & Matos, 2018). In rioting – when these dynamics occur as single time-limited events – there are enough protestors or police radicalised to see a breakdown in the social contract that protects peaceful dissent.

The risk of state radicalisation towards repression beyond any single incident becomes higher, by definition, as the norms and institutions of democracy weaken and are undermined. In this case, protestors as well as state leaders and authorities may move up a continuum from disorderly protests or riots to coercive surveillance and state repression of peaceful activism, protestor subversiveness and disregard for the law, and even insurgency and revolution (Crelinsten, 2002; Moghaddam, 2018; Pratt, 2015). It seems to us that this process, of radicalisation to the point that violence by state actors is tolerated and the rule of law is ignored, may occur within any given arena of collective action – for example, legitimising corporate sanctioned violence against environmental groups (Global Witness, 2018). Investigation into strategies for effective deradicalisation of state and corporate actors, including effective non-violent collective action responses, deserves research attention and would have substantial applied value.

6.5 The Impact of State Repression on Activists

In the absence of any effective deradicalisation strategies for state actors, many activists have faced the reality that when the opponent holds a monopoly on power, or is asymmetrically stronger, that opponent can also choose to repress protest. The techniques of repression can include free speech restrictions, intimidation, censorship, torture, and political imprisonment, aiming to ensure the continuity of the regime and prevent mobilisation (Carey, 2006; Davenport, 2000, 2007). Some research has shown that repressive action may indeed suppress activism, by instilling fear and raising the perceived costs to social movement actors (Ellefsen, 2016). Yet consistent with what we have seen for protestors, state repression has also sometimes been found to increase mobilisation (Anisin, 2016).

Comparatively limited analysis of protest in repressive contexts has been carried out, but this work suggests that activists' motives for collective action in repressive states are defined by moral considerations more strongly than instrumental considerations (Orazani & Leidner, 2019). Collective action to challenge state repression has also been linked to support from interpersonal and international networks (Siegel, 2011). Other scholars have found that repression generates greater anger and greater perceived effectiveness of protest to express activists' values, resulting in greater collective action intentions via both of those paths (Ayanian & Tausch, 2016). Sometimes, as in Box 9, it has been observed that activists' tactical repertoires change as they are channelled into the narrower range permitted by the repressive state, such as legal challenges (Chua, 2012) or literature and art (e.g., Jasper, 1997).

However, the impact of state repression is not only in limiting or triggering protest by activists, but also in its effects on state actors in creating norms for state impunity, corruption, and coerciveness that slow or prevent lasting social change. Case studies of revolutions and other forms of violent collective action suggest that the lack of political plasticity in polarised or authoritarian societies can corrupt multiple actors (Wagoner, Moghaddam, & Valsiner, 2018). For example, collective action may lead to regime change, but new leaders may continue to enforce authoritarian policies, and to exploit the citizens and resources of the repressive state (Moghaddam, 2013, 2016). According to the

BOX 9 THE TIBETAN INDEPENDENCE MOVEMENT AND STATE REPRESSION

Tibetans have long used non-violent resistance in their quest for independence (Dorjee, 2015). Across three movement waves, tactics changed from a predominantly violent first uprising (1956–9), to localised non-violent action (1987–9), to a third wave of non-violent action from 2008 which was more geographically dispersed. The third wave focused on China as an opponent, seeking to convert views and values through third parties' diplomatic pressure, despite attempts by China to eradicate any signs of Tibetan dissent. The impact of repression, according to Dorjee (2015), has been to move resistance into new tactical repertoires such as non-cooperation (i.e., refusing to support Chinese businesses) and alternative forms of civil resistance such as the promotion of the Tibetan language. Tibetans are argued to have changed their repertoire of tactics to de-collectivise their activism: examples given by Dorjee include small acts of resistance held every Wednesday, such as wearing traditional clothes and using Tibetan language at home.

In the Tibetan context, non-violent leadership has been provided by leaders such as the Dalai Lama (Dorjee, 2015). The use of non-violence was questioned by some activist factions in the 1960s and 1970s, particularly given violent political repression such as the burning of monasteries and disrobing of Tibetan monks and nuns. However, little radicalisation to violence has occurred. One striking exception is the practice of self-immolation, with more than 100 Tibetans committing the act since 2009. This practice, positioned by Chinese authorities as terrorism, has been associated with increased security and surveillance in protest regions. Given the consistent commitment of Tibetans to non-violence, and their lack of success in gaining independence, some scholars suggest that the Tibetan movement calls into question whether non-violent resistance has been an effective response to repression (Kohn, 2014).

work of Chenoweth and colleagues, it is non-violent action mobilising a significant minority of the population that has the capacity to result in transformative change (Chenoweth & Lewis, 2013; Stephan & Chenoweth, 2008). Why might this be the case?

One theoretical analysis is that in mutual radicalisation (Louis et al., 2020; Moghaddam, 2018) or 'co-radicalisation' (Crelinsten, 2002; Pratt, 2015), as we have discussed, state authorities and protestors risk becoming characterised by a mutual fixation on the other side's extremists, and a developing blindness to the other side's moderates. Each side then successively escalates its own radical positions to confront the illegitimate and threatening extremists. Other groups' use of lawbreaking or terrorism legitimises (some) police and politicians' contempt and willingness to abrogate human rights. Contempt from (some) agents of the state, and human rights abuses, legitimise (some) protestors' contempt for the authorities, and willingness to subvert the law, and to undermine the state. And so it goes on.

In this context, it is clear that one element of an ineffective transition frame towards democracy is a 'diagnosis' of the problem of the previous state corruption and repression as caused by the previous elite and leadership. As Moghaddam has argued in a series of books on the psychology of democratic and authoritarian societies (Moghaddam, 2013, 2016, 2018), there are always would-be dictators in the wings, waiting for the 'springboard to power' to transform democratic societies. Thus, it is institutions and cultures of democracy at the macro and micro level that sustain democracy and prevent authoritarianism and corruption.

It is at this point that we see the importance of understanding the actions of other groups within arenas for any given political context (see also Louis et al., 2018). At the macro level, independent judiciaries, lawyers, and police are required to support the rule of law; education systems are required to support voters committed to democratic oversight; and anti-corruption laws and policies are required to limit enmeshment of politicians with industry. At the micro level, norms or political skills are required to promote mutual respect, openness, and compromise to engage minorities and constrain elite power, and intolerance of intolerance is required to stem the group processes that otherwise reward polarisation and escalation. Just as all of these fall in concert, like dominoes, all may need to be rebuilt in concert: a frail house of cards with each layer depending on support from the others. The implication is that activists focused on any one arena or issue alone will thus not be able to sustain the transformation of the whole system. They must create coalitions that move all of the pieces in concert, while resisting the counter-mobilisation and repression of their opponents. However, it would be fair to say that these contentions rest on little concrete empirical research, given that the scholarship of the relationship between macro-level changes and collective action is still in its infancy (Louis & Montiel, 2018; Smith, Livingstone, & Thomas, 2019).

This section has focused on providing an overview of the dynamics of third parties and arenas and considering their importance in analyses of effective collective action. While we have highlighted the value of delineating arenas and the interactions between them, much remains to be uncovered regarding the processes that allow political polarisation, gridlock, and breakthroughs, acting across levels from individual and group to arena and coalition.

Longitudinal research to examine effective collective action, policy changes, and influences on counter-mobilisation would be particularly valuable. In the following final section, we bring together a research agenda for each of the components we have considered in turn, before concluding with a set of key takeaways.

7 Agenda for Future Research

This Element has analysed the social psychology of effective collective action. We have highlighted where the knowledge rests, and how the existing and novel scholarship and theorising applies to the different groups. In this final section we introduce a brief suggested research agenda for understanding the social psychology of effective activism for each of our audiences. We then highlight key take-home messages for those interested in achieving effective activism.

As a general point, we would comment that there are few studies that examine the impact of collective action simultaneously on supporters, bystanders, opponents, and third parties, or that explore how collective action impacts and is impacted by changes in the structure of democratic societies. Given the polarising forces at play around the world, and the immense challenges such as climate change that are not being effectively addressed at present, it is to be hoped that such research will be progressed sooner rather than later.

Table 2 summarises key questions for each of the areas for future research. Work on each of these future research components will assist in better understanding the psychological processes that will lead to effective collective action outcomes.

7.1 Self and Supporters

In Section 3, we focused on well-established drivers that motivate individuals to engage in collective action: factors such as identities, norms, moral conviction, efficacy, anger, and perceived injustice, along with individual difference variables. This research is important, but one question is highly salient and remains largely unanswered: what about longer-term engagement? Many activists drop out of social movements; why do some continue their participation over the longer term? Why do some become leaders or organisers? We know comparatively little about the specific factors and processes that differentiate between activists who drop out, those who persist, and those who step up to lead.

Turning to a different point for research with supporters, only briefly touched on in this Element, we note that the growing influence of online platforms in collective action practice warrants further investigation. These platforms

Table 2 Areas for future research.

Component	Questions for future research
Self and supporters	What factors influence engagement in sustained participation in collective action, and organising/leadership?
	What are the factors influencing the effectiveness of online collective action in generating participation, sustained participation, and leadership in collective action?
Bystanders	What effect does framing (e.g., inclusive or oppositional) have on bystander responses to activists and collective action?
	What are the risks and protective factors linked to bystander radicalisation?
Opponents	What processes support opponents to become allies?
	What are the risks and protective factors linked to opponent counter-mobilisation and radicalisation?
	What factors and processes create opponent deradicalisation?
Third parties	What factors and processes influence the formation of coalitions and alleviation of policy 'gridlock'?
	What factors and processes allow a cycle of mutual radicalisation to be arrested?

connect and organise greater numbers of people (Bimber, Flanagin & Stohl, 2012), significantly increasing the capacity of activists to reach more potential supporters, as well as offering more opportunity to grassroots, loosely organised, or even ephemeral collectives to organise collective action (Vehlken, 2013). We have suggested in Section 3 that online action may play an important role in building awareness and sympathy, creating a supporter opinion group identity, and a pool of supporters who may then be available for mobilisation in the ABIASCA framework. Other research has identified specific psychological traits that may be linked to those who organise online collective action and those who follow or support it (Margetts, John, Hale, & Reissfelder, 2015), as well as examining the role of efficacy and identity in supporting online action (Alberici & Milesi, 2016). Further research on the means by which online collective action is effective in gaining new supporters and sustaining persistent activists, and its relationship with offline action, will continue to be of great value (e.g., Thomas et al., 2015). The ubiquitous nature of online collective action also is creating new, unparalleled opportunity for collecting the big data over time that might allow scholars to map the links between awareness, sympathy, intentions, and action, not to mention 'persisting to power' with coalition building and sustained engagement in the face of counter-mobilisation. This is an exciting direction for future research.

7.2 Bystanders

Section 4 focused on the challenges involved in attracting bystanders to mobilise for a cause. In particular, we considered the role of agenda setting, public opinion, and perceived relevance in raising bystander awareness of issues. We also considered how bystander sympathy can be generated through the mechanism of supportive framing, by fostering the development of new identities, relationships, and connections with activists and activist groups. This section also briefly touched on different motives for bystander mobilisation, such as allyship and solidarity.

In general, there is limited research accounting for the diversity of bystanders' motives, actions, and experiences as they join or fail to join collective action, whether in favour of disadvantaged groups, or seeking to preserve the status quo. In our analysis of effective mobilisation of bystanders, however, we have spent proportionately less time on how activists seeking to entrench their own group's power and status relate to bystanders (Louis, Duck, Terry, & Lalonde, 2010), or how 'lone wolf' actors, acting alone on behalf of a real or imagined group (Moskalenko & McCauley, 2011), would engage or imagine the bystander audience. We acknowledge these as directions of research that deserve attention.

It is also clear that there is a vast arsenal of tactics of intimidation and deterrence that activists seeking domination might deploy, whether in seeking to elicit appeasement, avoidance, or active collaboration from the bystander group. Collective action and framing exercises directed at establishing limits on acceptable action, and positioning bystanders as outsiders, seeking to demobilise them from acting, have also received comparatively little research attention. We look forward to a future social psychology which grapples more directly with the operation and impact of this type of activist and collective action frame.

Looking at tactics, there is also an interesting nuance concerning bystanders' risks of radicalisation that has not, to our knowledge, been explored by psychologists. Specifically, we know from the literature on religious terrorism that converts are at much greater risk of being recruited towards violent extremism, compared to those raised in a faith: up to ten times higher (e.g., Simcox, Stuart, & Ahmed, 2010). It seems a plausible hypothesis that for any movement, it may be paradoxically easier for radical factions to recruit bystanders than members of their own constituencies. The bystanders enter the movement as people who are developing a commitment to the cause without having the internalised values and norms of the movement itself. Thus, in principle, bystanders would be more open to the movement fringes, and less committed to norms that promote conventional or peaceful action. However, to our knowledge little research has addressed this question empirically.

7.3 Opponents

In Section 5 we considered how activists can effectively overcome the opponents' barriers and exploit their weaknesses. We first highlighted the importance of defining opponents in narrow terms, enabling the identification of factions or constituents who may be more easily influenced. These factions can be drawn into inclusive identity categories, potentially transforming from an opponent to a supporter. The processes involved in transforming opponents into allies are worthy of detailed future research.

Section 5 also considered the challenge of avoiding radicalisation. Radicalisation and deradicalisation processes are fruitful areas for future research, given the comparatively limited empirical data currently available. For example, there are a few small group studies of protestors' discussions around radicalising from normative actions (Jimenez-Moya et al., 2015; Tausch et al., 2011; Thomas et al., 2014; Webber et al., 2017); there are none to our knowledge examining state actors' radicalisation, or small groups of radical actors talking about deradicalisation. What actions, if any, of activists are more likely to feature in opponents' narratives of radicalisation and deradicalisation? How do activists' choices constrain or alter the leadership contests of opponents, and change the dynamics of opponents' factionalism? These questions would benefit from scholars' attention. As a broader point, there are comparatively few studies examining non-WEIRD (Western, Educated, Industrialised, Rich, and Democratic) contexts and, in particular, repressive states. How do the attitudes and actions of activists towards third parties and opponents change as authoritarianism or democratic norms grow?

7.4 Third Parties

In Section 6 we considered the social psychological processes linked to engaging three third-party groups: activists for other causes, the media, and policymakers. This section highlighted the influence that support – obtained through coalition building, and selecting tactics which maximise supportive media coverage – from these third parties can have on collective action outcomes. This section also considered the problem of policy gridlock, where entrenched positions can facilitate counter-mobilisation, or in some scenarios, the radicalisation of state actors towards repression and authoritarianism.

We suggest two research agendas for better understanding how activists can gain third-party support, or suffer from oppositional coalitions. As highlighted in Section 6, the macro-level dynamics of activists and the groups they interact with have been the subject of a rich tradition of research looking at the outcomes of social movements and arenas of contestation. However, connecting these outcomes with social psychological processes, particularly around breaking policy gridlock, would greatly assist research in this complex area. Concurrently, investigating and identifying specific psychological drivers associated with support or opposition to collective action and coalition building from the perspective of different third-party group members would considerably help better understanding these processes.

Research questions could, for example, investigate what identities, norms, actions, emotions, and beliefs of actors allow gridlock to be broken, by the recruiting of new members into a coalition and by the unfreezing of a formerly solid alliance. This work will also assist in identifying links between policy gridlock and polarisation at various levels of analysis, from societal norms of democracy or repression to group norms of partisanship and factionalism to individual sentiments of antipathy and contempt.

In addition, we return to the point that mobilisation and counter-mobilisation are dynamic and complex processes, particularly when movements seek to engage multiple third parties across long periods of time (e.g., the environmental movement). Many of these movements are working towards transformative systems change. However, it is fair to say that empirical research on processes of system change is comparatively recent and the field is growing rapidly (Louis, 2009; Louis & Montiel, 2018; Louis et al., 2020; Moghaddam, 2018; Smith et al., 2019). We look forward with great enthusiasm to future research which directly addresses the mechanisms of effective and ineffective system change attempts. In this area we also suggest analysis of the factors and processes at the individual, group, and intergroup level which can allow a cycle of mutual radicalisation to be arrested. We have argued that sometimes when the likelihood of systems change is low, activists and their groups may innovate to move towards more non-normative tactical repertoires, prompting more radical responses from third parties and opponents in turn. Corrupt and violent state actors, and the citizens who offer them norms of silence and impunity, also invite psychologists' attention. Using the DIME model in empirical applications – that is, exploring how activists respond to perceptions of failure and success (Lizzio-Wilson et al., 2021; Louis et al., 2020) – may be valuable to shed light on the social psychological processes involved in this dynamic.

As a general comment, it seems to us that there are a great number of 'low-hanging fruit' in relation to effective activism that simply await researchers' time, energy, and resources. There are comparatively little empirical data that have considered dynamics between activists and third parties, that have examined state actors, or that have looked across levels of analysis and across parties to see identities and norms changing within an arena as conflict escalates. Case studies as well as longitudinal surveys and experimental data will be of great value.

7.5 Take-Home Messages

Our first take-home message is to focus on the diversity of actors, audiences, and goals as presented in the ABIASCA framework (Section 2). Supporters, bystanders, opponents, and third parties represent different actors as well as audiences of collective action, inviting different tactical choices as well as considerations of effectiveness. For example, orienting to bystanders, activists should think about building awareness and sympathy, and generating intentions to participate in action for the cause. On the other hand, activists might think about defeating opponents in the 'battlefield' by creating message frames that will grow coalitions, or managing the dangers of mutual radicalisation.

Our second take-home message is to consider the impact of failure. In the DIME model reviewed in Section 2 (Lizzio-Wilson et al., 2021; Louis et al., 2020), failure feedback for collective action is seen as a prompt that can create diverging trajectories among activists, with some dropping out, others innovating, and others gaining more moral conviction and energy. Since experiences of failure and success are highly contested and variable, these dynamics reinforce the volatility of collective action.

Third, as we have seen, the journey of collective action does not only involve in-groups (us, supporters) and out-groups (they/them, opponents), but also bystanders who have not decided their position, and third parties who may reinforce or attenuate the effectiveness of the collective action, and change the identities and positions being contested. In the longer term, persisting and creating political solidarity to include majorities in broader coalitions (building support from bystanders and third parties, outside the binary of supporter–opponent conflict on any one issue) is important for influencing authorities and creating the desired changes.

Our final take-home message seeks to highlight the importance of a nuanced understanding of opponents. The dynamics of supporters versus opponents can certainly be understood as a binary opposition, in which when the one wins, the other is defeated. However, as we have seen, activists who are supporters and opponents work in large arenas of cooperation and contest across multiple issues. Opponents on one issue may be allies in the future, or for other issues, and may cooperate (or not) in sustaining more democratic and open societies. Moreover, at the same time as they manage the intergroup conflict with each other, both opponents and supporters may also struggle to manage internal contests in which moderate and extremist factions within each group seek to shape the group's norms. A broader analysis of the dynamic of activists, opponents, bystanders, and third parties, and their roles in undermining or affirming democracy, seems at the present time as though it would be profitable to scholars and activists alike.

7.6 Conclusion

This Element focused on examining the social psychology of effective activism. Specifically, we explored the diversity of understandings of effectiveness, identifying how conceptualisations of effectiveness may differ according to activists' different instrumental and symbolic goals, the collective action tactics they choose to achieve these goals, and the particular audiences to which collective action is directed.

Understanding these processes has important theoretical and practical consequences. Collective action and new social movements are prevalent across most nations in the twenty-first century, fostered by increasing online activism, and rising concern around issues as diverse as the looming climate crisis, immigration, and political authoritarianism. As highlighted in this Element, collective action seeking to address these concerns can certainly facilitate solutions, but also foster stalemates and polarising conflict. To help achieve the former, in Table 2 we have highlighted two research questions for each of the four collective action audiences that the social psychological literature could address. Most importantly, we stress three focal areas for consideration: the need for considering each of these four audience perspectives in social psychological analyses of collective action; further investigating the processes related to failure; and expanding our conceptualisations and understanding of opponents in the collective action field.

While much is known regarding the psychological processes related to effective activism, particularly in relation to mobilisation of self and supporters, it is clear that important questions remain to be addressed. This Element highlights a growing literature on the social psychology of effective activism and celebrates its potential to help to provide insights into one of humanity's most powerful mechanisms for creating social change. In closing, we invite our readers to join us in a collective endeavour to bring forward this scholarship – or to join us in an open dialogue of active dissent.

References

Aalberg, T., Esser, F., Reinemann, C., Stromback, J., & De Vreese, C. (2016). *Populist Political Communication in Europe*. New York: Routledge.

Agnone, J. (2007). Amplifying public opinion: The policy impact of the US environmental movement. *Social Forces, 85*(4), 1593–620. www.jstor.org/stable/4495000

Agronick, G. S., & Duncan, L. E. (1998). Personality and social change: Individual differences, life path, and importance attributed to the women's movement. *Journal of Personality and Social Psychology, 74*(6), 1545–1555. https://doi.org/10.1037/0022-3514.74.6.1545

Ajzen, I. (1991). The theory of planned behavior. *Organizational Behavior and Human Decision Processes, 50*(2), 179–211.

Alberici, A. I., & Milesi, P. (2016). Online discussion, politicized identity, and collective action. *Group Processes and Intergroup Relations, 19*(1), 43–59. https://doi.org/10.1177/1368430215581430

Anderson, M., & Hitlin, P. (2016). Social media conversations about race: How social media users see, share and discuss race and the rise of hashtags like #BlackLivesMatter. Retrieved from: www.pewresearch.org/internet/2016/08/15/social-media-conversations-about-race.

Andits, P. (2016). From historical injustice to local conflict: Mobilization–counter-mobilization dynamics surrounding the 2005 Melbourne 'Trianon Protest'. *Social Movement Studies, 15*(3), 322–34. https://doi.org/10.1080/14742837.2015.1070727

Andrews, K., & Caren, N. (2010). Making the news: Movement organizations, media attention, and the public agenda. *American Sociological Review, 75*(6), 841–66. https://doi.org/10.1177/0003122410386689

Anisin, A. (2016). Violence begets violence: Why states should not lethally repress popular protest. *The International Journal of Human Rights, 20*(7), 893–913. https://doi.org/10.1080/13642987.2016.1192536

Art, D. (2011). *Inside the Radical Right: The Development of Anti-Immigrant Parties in Western Europe*. Cambridge: Cambridge University Press.

Awad, S. H. (2016). The identity process in times of rupture: Narratives from the Egyptian revolution. *Journal of Social and Political Psychology, 4*(1), 128–41. https://doi.org/10.5964/jspp.v4i1.521

Ayanian, A. H., & Tausch, N. (2016). How risk perception shapes collective action intentions in repressive contexts: A study of Egyptian activists during the 2013 post-coup uprising. *British Journal of Social Psychology*, *55*(4), 700–21. https://doi.org/10.1111/bjso.12164

Baggetta, M., Han, H., & Andrews, K. T. (2013). Leading associations: How individual characteristics and team dynamics generate committed leaders. *American Sociological Review*, *78*(4), 544–73. https://doi.org/10.1177 /0003122413489877

Bain, P. G., Hornsey, M. J., Bongiorno, R., Kashima, Y., & Crimston, D. (2013). Collective futures: How projections about the future of society are related to actions and attitudes supporting social change. *Personality and Social Psychology Bulletin*, *39*(4), 523–39.

Bamberg, S., Rees, J., & Seebauer, S. (2015). Collective climate action: Determinants of participation intention in community-based pro-environmental initiatives. *Journal of Environmental Psychology*, *43*, 155–65. http://dx.doi.org/10.1016/j.jenvp.2015.06.006

Bandura, A. (2000). Exercise of human agency through collective efficacy. *Current Directions in Psychological Science*, *9*(3), 75–8. www.jstor.org /stable/20182630

Bar-Tal, D. (2000). From intractable conflict through conflict resolution to reconciliation: Psychological analysis. *Political Psychology*, *21*(2), 351–65. www.jstor.org/stable/3791795

Beamish, T. D., & Luebbers, A. J. (2009). Alliance building across social movements: Bridging difference in a peace and justice coalition. *Social Problems*, *56*(4), 647–76. https://doi.org/10.1525/sp.2009.56.4.647

Beer, M. (2021). *Revisiting the Methods of Nonviolent Action*. Washington, DC: International Center on Nonviolent Conflict.

Ben David, Y., & Rubel-Lifschitz, T. (2018). Practice the change you want to see in the world: Transformative practices of social movements in Israel. *Peace and Conflict: Journal of Peace Psychology*, *24*(1), 10–18.

Benford, R. D., & Snow, D. A. (2000). Framing processes and social movements: An overview and assessment. *Annual Review of Sociology*, *26*, 611–39. www.jstor.org/stable/223459

Bennett, W. L., & Iyengar, S. (2008). A new era of minimal effects? The changing foundations of political communication. *Journal of Communication*, *58*(4), 707–31. https://doi.org/10.1111/j.1460-2466 .2008.00410.x

Berndsen, M., Thomas, E. F., & Pedersen, A. (2018). Resisting perspective-taking: Glorification of the national group elicits non-compliance with perspective-taking instructions. *Journal of Experimental Social Psychology*, *79*, 126–37. https://doi.org/10.1016/j .jesp.2018.07.007

Bimber, B., Flanagin, A., & Stohl, C. (2012). *Collective Action in Organizations: Interaction and Engagement in an Era of Technological Change*. Cambridge, UK: Cambridge University Press.

Blackwood, L., & Louis, W. R. (2017). Choosing between conciliatory and oppositional leaders: The role of out-group signals and in-group leader candidates' collective action tactics. *European Journal of Social Psychology*, *47*(3), 320–36. https://doi.org/10.1002/ejsp.2249

Blackwood, L. M., & Louis, W. R. (2012). If it matters for the group then it matters to me: Collective action outcomes for seasoned activists. *British Journal of Social Psychology*, *51*(1), 72–92. https://doi.org/10.1111/j.2044 -8309.2010.02001.x

Bliuc, A.M., McGarty, C., Hartley, L., & Muntele H.D. (2012). Manipulating national identity: The strategic use of rhetoric by supporters and opponents of the 'Cronulla riots' in Australia. *Ethnic and Racial Studies*, *35*(12), 2174–94. https://doi.org/10.1080/01419870.2011.600768

Bliuc, A.M., McGarty, C., Thomas, E. F., Lala, G., Berndsen, M., & Misajon, R. (2015). Public division about climate change rooted in conflicting socio-political identities. *Nature Climate Change*, *5*(3), 226–9. https://doi .org/10.1038/nclimate2507

Bliuc, A. M., McGarty, C., & Reynolds, K. (2003). Predicting political behaviour in opinion-based groups: The role of social identification and social identity salience. *Australian Journal of Psychology*, *55*, 34.

Bliuc, A. M., McGarty, C., Reynolds, K., & Muntele, D. (2007). Opinion-based group membership as a predictor of commitment to political action. *European Journal of Social Psychology*, *37*(1), 19–32. https://doi.org/10 .1002/ejsp.334

Boin, A., 't Hart, P., & McConnell, A. (2009). Crisis exploitation: Political and policy impacts of framing contests. *Journal of European Public Policy*, *16*(1), 81–106. https://doi.org/10.1080/13501760802453221

Bongiorno, R., McGarty, C., Kurz, T., Haslam, S. A., & Sibley, C. G. (2016). Mobilizing cause supporters through group-based interaction. *Journal of Applied Social Psychology*, *46*(4), 203–15. https://doi.org/10.1111/jasp.12337

Boscarino, J. E. (2016). Setting the record straight: Frame contestation as an advocacy tactic. *Policy Studies Journal*, *44*(3), 280–308. https://doi.org/10 .1111/psj.12121

Bowles, S., & Gintis, H. (2011). *A Cooperative Species: Human Reciprocity and Its Evolution*. Princeton, NJ: Princeton University Press.

Bradley, B. (2011). The rise and decline of Australian unionism: A history of Industrial labour from the 1820s to 2010. *Labour History*, *100*, 51–82. https:// doi.org/10.5263/labourhistory.100.0051

Burstein, P. (1998). Bringing the public back in: Should sociologists consider the impact of public opinion on public policy? *Social Forces, 77*(1), 27–62. https://doi.org/10.2307/3006009

Burstein, P. (2003). The impact of public opinion on public policy: A review and an agenda. *Political Research Quarterly, 56*(1), 29–40. www.jstor.org/stable/3219881

Caiani, M., & Della Porta, D. (2018). The radical right as social movement organizations. In J. Rydgren (ed.), *The Oxford Handbook of the Radical Right.* Oxford: Oxford University Press, 52–80. https://doi.org/10.1093/oxfordhb/9780190274559.001.0001

Canetti-Nisim, D., Halperin, E., Sharvit, K., & Hobfoll, S. E. (2009). A new stress-based model of political extremism: Personal exposure to terrorism, psychological distress, and exclusionist political attitudes. *Journal of Conflict Resolution, 53*(3), 363–89. https://doi.org/10.1177/0022002709333296

Canetti, D., Hall, B. J., Rapaport, C., & Wayne, C. (2013). Exposure to political violence and political extremism. *European Psychologist, 18*(4), 263–72. https://doi.org/10.1027/1016-9040/a000158

Carey, S. C. (2006). The dynamic relationship between protest and repression. *Political Research Quarterly, 59*(1), 1–11. https://doi.org/10.1177/106591290605900101

Carman, J. G., & Nesbit, R. (2013). Founding new nonprofit organizations: Syndrome or symptom? *Nonprofit and Voluntary Sector Quarterly, 42*(3), 603–21. https://doi.org/10.1177/0899764012459255

Chen, C. W., & Gorski, P. C. (2015). Burnout in social justice and human rights activists: Symptoms, causes and implications. *Journal of Human Rights Practice, 7*(3), 366–90. https://doi.org/10.1093/jhuman/huv011

Chenoweth, E. (2020). The future of nonviolent resistance. *Journal of Democracy, 31*(3), 69–84.

Chenoweth, E., & Lewis, O. A. (2013). Unpacking nonviolent campaigns: Introducing the NAVCO 2.0 dataset. *Journal of Peace Research, 50*(3), 415–23. https://doi.org/10.1177/0022343312471551

Chenoweth, E., & Stephan, M. J. (2011). *Why Civil Resistance Works: The Strategic Logic of Non-Violent Conflict.* New York: Columbia University Press.

Chua, L. J. (2012). Pragmatic resistance, law, and social movements in authoritarian states: The case of gay collective action in Singapore. *Law and Society Review, 46*(4), 713–48. https://doi.org/10.1111/j.1540-5893.2012.00515.x

Cordner, A., Brown, P., & Mulcahy, M. (2015). Playing with fire: Flame retardant activists and policy arenas. In J. W. Duyvendak & J. Jasper (eds). *Players and Arenas: The Interactive Dynamics of Protest.* Amsterdam: Amsterdam University Press, 211–28.

Crelinsten, R. D. (2002). Analysing terrorism and counter-terrorism: A communication model. *Terrorism and political violence*, *14*(2), 77–122. https://doi.org/10.1080/714005618

Cress, D. M., & Snow, D. A. (2000). The outcomes of homeless mobilization: The influence of organization, disruption, political mediation, and framing. *American Journal of Sociology*, *105*(4), 1063–104. https://www.jstor.org/stable/3003888

Curtin, N., Kende, A., & Kende, J. (2016). Navigating multiple identities: The simultaneous influence of advantaged and disadvantaged identities on politicization and activism. *Journal of Social Issues*, *72*(2), 264–85. https://doi.org/10.1111/josi.12166

Curtin, N., & McGarty, C. (2016). Expanding on psychological theories of engagement to understand activism in context(s). *Journal of Social Issues*, *72*(2), 227–41. https://doi.org/10.1111/josi.12164

Danaher, K., & Branscombe, N. R. (2010). Maintaining the system with tokenism: Bolstering individual mobility beliefs and identification with a discriminatory organization. *British Journal of Social Psychology*, *49*(2), 343–62. https://doi.org/10.1348/014466609X457530

Davenport, C. (2000). *Paths to State Repression: Human Rights Violations and Contentious Politics*. New York: Rowman & Littlefield Publishers.

Davenport, C. (2007). State repression and political order. *Annual Review of Political Science*, *10*, 1–23. https://doi.org/10.1146/annurev.polisci.10.101405.143216

Dearing, J. W., & Rogers, E. M. (1996). *Communication Concept 6: Agenda-Setting*. London: Sage Publications.

Della Porta, D., & Rucht, D. (1995). Left-libertarian movements in context: A comparison of Italy and West Germany, 1965–1990. *Discussion Paper FS III 91–102*. Berlin: Wissenschaftszentrum.

Digman, J. M. (1990). Personality structure: Emergence of the five-factor model. *Annual Review of Psychology*, *41*(1), 417–40. https://doi.org/10.1146/annurev.ps.41.020190.002221

Dixon, J., & Levine, M. (2012). *Beyond Prejudice: Extending the Social Psychology of Conflict, Inequality and Social Change*. Cambridge: Cambridge University Press.

Dobbin, F., & Jung, J. (2015). Professions, social movements, and the sovereign corporation. In J. M. Jasper & J. W. Duyvendak (eds.), *Players and Arenas: The Interactive Dynamics of Protest*. Amsterdam: Amsterdam University Press.

Dodge, J. (2016). Crowded advocacy: Framing dynamic in the fracking controversy in New York. *Voluntas: International Journal of Voluntary and*

Nonprofit Organizations, *28*(3), 888–915. https://doi.org/10.1007/s11266-016-9800-6

Dorjee, T. (2015). *The Tibetan Nonviolent Struggle: A Strategic and Historical Analysis*. Washington, DC: International Center on Nonviolent Conflict.

Doucerain, M., Amiot, C. E., Thomas, E., & Louis, W. R. (2018). What it means to be American: Identity inclusiveness/exclusiveness and support for policies about Muslims among U.S.-born Whites. *Analyses of Social Issues and Public Policy*, *18*(1), 224–43. https://doi.org/10.1111/asap.12167

Downton Jr, J., & Wehr, P. (1998). Persistent pacifism: How activist commitment is developed and sustained. *Journal of Peace Research*, *35*(5), 531–50. https://doi.org/10.1177/0022343398035005001

Droogendyk, L., Wright, S. C., Lubensky, M., & Louis, W. R. (2016). Acting in solidarity: Cross-group contact between disadvantaged group members and advantaged group allies. *Journal of Social Issues*, *72*(2), 315–34. https://doi.org/10.1111/josi.12168

Drury, J., Cocking, C., Beale, J., Hanson, C., & Rapley, F. (2005). The phenomenology of empowerment in collective action. *British Journal of Social Psychology*, *44*, 309–28. https://doi.org/10.1348/014466604x18523

Drury, J., & Reicher, S. (2000). Collective action and psychological change: The emergence of new social identities. *British Journal of Social Psychology*, *39*(4), 579–604. https://doi.org/10.1348/014466600164642

Drury, J., & Reicher, S. (2005). Explaining enduring empowerment: A comparative study of collective action and psychological outcomes. *European Journal of Social Psychology*, *35*(1), 35–58. https://doi.org/10.1002/ejsp.231

Drury, J., & Reicher, S. (2009). Collective psychological empowerment as a model of social change: Researching crowds and power. *Journal of Social Issues*, *65*(4), 707–25. https://doi.org/10.1111/j.1540-4560.2009.01622.x

Drury, J., Stott, C., & Farsides, T. (2003). The role of police perceptions and practices in the development of 'public disorder'. *Journal of Applied Social Psychology*, *33*(7), 1480–1500. https://doi.org/10.1111/j.1559-1816.2003.tb01959.x

Duncan, L. E. (1999). Motivation for collective action: Group consciousness as mediator of personality, life experiences, and women's rights activism. *Political Psychology*, *20*(3), 611–35. https://doi.org/10.1111/0162-895X.00159

Duncan, L. E. (2012). The Psychology of collective action. In K. Deaux & M. Snyder (eds.), *The Oxford Handbook of Personality and Social Psychology*. Oxford: Oxford University Press.

Dupuis, D. R., Wohl, M. J., Packer, D. J., & Tabri, N. (2016). To dissent and protect: Stronger collective identification increases willingness to dissent when group norms evoke collective angst. *Group Processes and Intergroup Relations*, *19*(5), 694–710. https://doi.org/10.1177/1368430216638535

Duyvendak, J. W., & Jasper, J. M. (2015). *Players and Arenas: The Interactive Dynamics of Protest*. Amsterdam: Amsterdam University Press.

Edwards, B., & McCarthy, J. D. (2004). Resources and social movement mobilization. In D. A. Snow, S. A. Soule, & H. Kriesi (eds.), *The Blackwell Companion to Social Movements*. New Jersey: Blackwell Publishing Ltd, 116–52. https://doi.org/10.1002/9780470999103.ch6

Edwards, B. , McCarthy, J. D., & Mataic, D. R. (2018). The resource context of social movements. In D. A. Snow, S. A. Soule, H. Kriesi, & H. J. McCammon (eds.), *The Wiley Blackwell Companion to Social Movements*. Hoboken, NJ: Wiley-Blackwell, 79–97.

Ellefsen, R. (2016). Judicial opportunities and the death of SHAC: Legal repression along a cycle of contention. *Social Movement Studies*, *15*(5), 441–56. https://doi.org/10.1080/14742837.2016.1185360

Ellefsen, R. (2018). Deepening the explanation of radical flank effects: Tracing contingent outcomes of destructive capacity. *Qualitative Sociology 41*(1), 111–33. https://doi.org/10.1007/s11133-018-9373-3

Entman, R. M. (1993). Framing: Toward clarification of a fractured paradigm. *Journal of Communication*, *43*, 51–8. https://doi.org/10.1111/j.1460-2466.1993.tb01304.x

Feinberg, M., Willer, R., & Kovacheff, C. (2020). The activist's dilemma: Extreme protest actions reduce popular support for social movements. *Journal of Personality and Social Psychology*, *119*(5), 1086–111. https://doi.org/10.1037/pspi0000230

Ferguson, N., McDaid, S., & McAuley, J. W. (2018). Social movements, structural violence, and conflict transformation in Northern Ireland: The role of loyalist paramilitaries. *Peace and Conflict: Journal of Peace Psychology*, *24*(1), 19–26. https://doi.org/10.1037/pac0000274

Ferree, M.M., & Mueller, C. (2004). Feminism and the women's movements: A global perspective. In D. A. Snow, S. A. Soule, & H. Kriesi (eds.), *The Blackwell Companion to Social Movements*. New Jersey: Blackwell Publishing, 116–52. https://doi.org/10.1002/9780470999103

Fetner, T. (2008). Taking to the streets: Protest and direct democracy. In T. Fetner (ed.), *How the Religious Right Shaped Lesbian and Gay Activism*. Minnesota: University of Minnesota Press. https://www.jstor.org/stable/10.5749/j.ctttvb8d

Fielding, K. S., & Hornsey, M. J. (2016). A social identity analysis of climate change and environmental attitudes and behaviors: Insights and opportunities. *Frontiers in Psychology, 7*, 121. https://doi.org/10.3389/fpsyg.2016.00121

Fielding, K.S., Hornsey, M.J., Thai, H.A., & Toh, L.L. (2019). Using ingroup messengers and ingroup values to promote climate change policy. *Climatic Change, 158*, 181–99. https://doi.org/10.1007/s10584-019-02561-z

Fielding, K. S., McDonald, R., & Louis, W. R. (2008). Theory of planned behaviour, identity and intentions to engage in environmental activism. *Journal of Environmental Psychology, 28*(4), 318–26. https://doi.org/10.1016/j.jenvp.2008.03.003

Flack, P., & Ferguson, N. (in press). Conflict transformation: Relinquishing or maintaining social identity among former loyalist combatants in Northern Ireland. *Political Psychology.* https://onlinelibrary.wiley.com/doi/abs/10.1111/pops.12694

Freudenberger, H. J. (1974). Staff burn-out. *Journal of Social Issues, 30*(1), 159–65. https://doi.org/10.1111/j.1540-4560.1974.tb00706.x

Fritsche, I., Barth, M., Jugert, P., Masson, T., & Reese, G. (2018). A social identity model of pro-environmental action (SIMPEA). *Psychological Review, 125*(2), 245–269.

Gallego, A., & Oberski, D. (2012). Personality and political participation: The mediation hypothesis. *Political Behavior, 34*(3), 425–51. https://doi.org/10.1007/s11109-011-9168-7

Gamson, W. A. (1992). *Talking Politics.* New York: Cambridge University Press.

Gamson, W. A., Fireman, B., & Rytina, S. (1982). *Encounters with Unjust Authority.* Belmont, CA: Dorsey Press.

Gattinara, P., & Pirro, A. L. (2019). The far right as social movement. *European Societies, 21*(4), 447–62. https://doi.org/10.1080/14616696.2018.1494301

Gerber, A. S., Huber, G. A., Doherty, D., & Dowling, C. M. (2011). The Big Five Personality traits in the political arena. *Annual Review of Political Science, 14*(1), 265–87. https://doi.org/10.1146/annurev-polisci-051010-111659

Giddings, P. J. (2009). *Ida A. Sword among Lions: Ida B. Wells and the Campaign Against Lynching.* New York: Harper Collins.

Giugni, M. (1998). Was it worth the effort? The outcomes and consequences of social movements. *Annual Review of Sociology, 24*(1), 371–93. https://doi.org/10.1146/annurev.soc.24.1.371

Global Witness (2018). *At What Cost? Irresponsible Business and the Murder of Land and Environmental Defenders in 2017.* London: Global Witness.

Glynn, C. J., & Huge, M. E. (2008). Public opinion. In *The International Encyclopedia of Communication*. New Jersey: John Wiley & Sons.

Goffman, E. (1974). *Frame Analysis: An Essay on the Organization of Experience*. Cambridge, MA: Harvard University Press.

Golder, M. (2016). Far right parties in Europe. *Annual Review of Political Science, 19*, 477–97. https://doi.org/10.1146/annurev-polisci-042814-012441

Gollwitzer, P. M., & Sheeran, P. (2006). Implementation intentions and goal achievement: A meta-analysis of effects and processes. *Advances in Experimental Social Psychology, 38*, 69–119.

Gomes, M. E. (1992). The rewards and stresses of social change: A qualitative study of peace activists. *Journal of Humanistic Psychology, 32*(4), 138–46. https://doi.org/10.1177/0022167892324008

Goodwin, J., & Pfaff, S. (2001). Emotion work in high-risk social movements: Managing fear in the US and East German civil rights movements. In J. Goodwin, J. M. Jasper, & F. Polletta (eds.), *Passionate Politics: Emotions and Social Movements*. Chicago: University of Chicago Press, 282–302. https://doi.org/10.7208/chicago/9780226304007.003.0017

Gordijn, E. H., de Vries, N. K., & de Dreu, C. K. W. (2002). Minority influence on focal and related attitudes: Change in size, attributions, and information processing. *Personality and Social Psychology Bulletin, 28*(10), 1315–26. https://doi.org/10.1177/014616702236819

Gouws, A., & Coetzee, A. (2019). Women's movements and feminist activism. *Agenda, 33*(2), 1–8. https://doi.org/10.1080/10130950.2019.1619263

Greenaway, K. H., Quinn, E. A., & Louis, W. R. (2011). Appealing to common humanity increases forgiveness but reduces collective action among victims of historical atrocities. *European Journal of Social Psychology, 41*(5), 569–73. https://doi.org/10.1002/ejsp.802

Gulliver, R., Chapman, C. M., Solly, K. N., & Schultz, T. (2020). Testing the impact of images in environmental campaigns. *Journal of Environmental Psychology, 71*, 101468. https://doi.org/10.1016/j.jenvp.2020.101468

Gulliver, R., Fielding, K. S., & Louis, W. R. (2019). Understanding the outcomes of climate change campaigns in the Australian environmental movement. *Case Studies in the Environment, 3*(1), 1–9. https://doi.org/10.1525/cse.2018.001651

Gulliver, R., Fielding, K. S., & Louis, W. (2020). The characteristics, activities and goals of environmental organizations engaged in advocacy within the Australian environmental movement. *Environmental Communication, 14*(5), 614–27. https://doi.org/10.1080/17524032.2019.1697326

Gusfield, J. R. (1986). *Symbolic Crusade: Status Politics and the American Temperance Movement*. Urbana and Chicago: University of Illinois Press.

Ha, S. E., Kim, S., & Jo, S. H. (2013). Personality traits and political participation: Evidence from South Korea. *Political Psychology*, *34*(4), 511–32. https://doi.org/10.1111/pops.12008

Haslam, S. A., Reicher, S. D., & Platow, M. J. (2010). *The New Psychology of Leadership: Identity, Influence and Power*. Milton Park:Taylor & Francis.

Hayward, L. E., Tropp, L. R., Hornsey, M. J., & Barlow, F. K. (2018). How negative contact and positive contact with Whites predict collective action among racial and ethnic minorities. *British Journal of Social Psychology*, *57* (1), 1–20. https://doi.org/10.1111/bjso.12220

Heinisch, R., & Mazzoleni, O. (2016). *Understanding Populist Party Organisation: The Radical Right in Western Europe*. London: Palgrave Macmillan.

Heumann, S., & Duyvendak, J. W. (2015). When and why religious groups become political players. In J. M. Jasper. & J. W. Duyvendak (eds.), *Players and Arenas: The Interactive Dynamics of Protest*. Amsterdam: Amsterdam University Press.

Hobolt, S., Leeper, T., & Tilley, J. (2020). Divided by the vote: Affective polarization in the wake of the Brexit referendum. *British Journal of Political Science*, 1–18. https://doi.org/10.1017/S0007123420000125

Hopgood, S. (2006). *Keepers of the Flame: Understanding Amnesty International*. New York: Cornell University Press.

Hopkins, N., Reicher, S. D., Khan, S. S., Tewari, S., Srinivasan, N., & Stevenson, C. (2016). Explaining effervescence: Investigating the relationship between shared social identity and positive experience in crowds. *Cognition and Emotion*, *30*(1), 20–32. https://doi.org/10.1080/02699931 .2015.1015969

Horgan, J. (2008). From profiles to pathways and roots to routes: Perspectives from psychology on radicalization into terrorism. *The ANNALS of the American Academy of Political and Social Science*, *618*(1), 80–94. https://doi .org/10.1177/0002716208317539

Horgan, J., Altier, M. B., Shortland, N., & Taylor, M. (2017). Walking away: The disengagement and de-radicalization of a violent right-wing extremist. *Behavioral Sciences of Terrorism and Political Aggression*, *9*(2), 63–77. https://doi.org/10.1080/19434472.2016.1156722

Hornsey, M. J., Blackwood, L., Louis, W., Fielding, K., Mavor, K., Morton, T., & White, K. M. (2006). Why do people engage in collective action? Revisiting the role of perceived effectiveness. *Journal of Applied Social Psychology*, *36* (7), 1701–22. https://doi.org/10.1111/j.0021-9029.2006.00077.x

Hornsey, M. J., Trembath, M., & Gunthorpe, S. (2004). 'You can criticize because you care': Identity attachment, constructiveness, and the intergroup sensitivity effect. *European Journal of Social Psychology, 34*(5), 499–518. https://doi.org/10.1002/ejsp.212

Hornung, J., Bandelow, N. C., & Vogeler, C. S. (2019). Social identities in the policy process. *Policy Sciences, 52*(2), 211–31. https://doi.org/10.1007/s11077-018-9340-6

Hoskin, R. E., Thomas, E. F., & McGarty, C. (2019). Transnational contact and challenging global poverty: Intergroup contact intensifies (the right kind of) social identities to promote solidarity-based collective action for those low in social dominance. *Journal of Theoretical Social Psychology, 3*(1), 23–34. https://doi.org/10.1002/jts5.24

Iyer, A., & Ryan, M. K. (2009). Why do men and women challenge gender discrimination in the workplace? The role of group status and in-group identification in predicting pathways to collective action. *Journal of Social Issues, 65*(4), 791–814. https://doi.org/10.1111/j.1540-4560.2009.01625.x

Jäckle, S., & König, P. D. (2017). The dark side of the German 'welcome culture': Investigating the causes behind attacks on refugees in 2015. *West European Politics, 40*(2), 223–51. https://doi.org/10.1080/01402382.2016.1215614

Jacobson, S. K., McDuff, M. D., & Monroe, M. C. (2015). *Conservation Education and Outreach Techniques*. Oxford: Oxford University Press.

Jacquet, J. (2017). Guilt and shame in US climate change communication. In *Oxford Research Encyclopedia of Climate Science*. Oxford: Oxford University Press.

Jasper, J. (2004). A strategic approach to collective action: Looking for agency in social-movement choices. *Mobilization: An International Quarterly, 9*(1), 1–16. https://doi.org/10.17813/maiq.9.1.m112677546p63361

Jasper, J. M. (1997). *The Art of Moral Protest: Culture, Biography, and Creativity in Social Movements*. Chicago: University of Chicago Press.

Jasper, J. M. (2019). Linking arenas: structuring concepts in the study of politics and protest. *Social Movement Studies*, 1–15. https://doi.org/10.1080/14742837.2019.1679106

Jenkins-Smith, H. C. (1990). *Democratic Politics and Policy Analysis*. Monterey County, CA: Brooks/Cole Publishing.

Jiménez-Moya, G., Spears, R., Rodríguez-Bailón, R., & de Lemus, S. (2015). By any means necessary? When and why low group identification paradoxically predicts radical collective action. *Journal of Social Issues, 71*(3), 517–35. https://doi.org/10.1111/josi.12126

Johnson, E.W., Agnone, J., & McCarthy, J.D. (2010). Movement organizations, synergistic tactics and environmental public policy. *Social Forces, 88*(5), 2267–92. https://doi.org/10.1353/sof.2010.0038

Jones, S. G., & Libicki, M. C. (2008). *How Terrorist Groups End: Lessons from Countering Al-Qa'ida*. London: RAND Corporation.

Jost, J. T., Becker, J., Osborne, D., & Badaan, V. (2017). Missing in (collective) action: Ideology, system justification, and the motivational antecedents of two types of protest behavior. *Current Directions in Psychological Science, 26*(2), 99–108. https://doi.org/10.1177/0963721417690633

Karácsony, G., & Róna, D. (2011). The secret of Jobbik: Reasons behind the rise of the Hungarian radical right. *Journal of East European & Asian Studies, 2* (1), 61–92.

Kidd, L. R., Garrard, G. E., Bekessy, S. A., Mills, M., Camilleri, A. R., Fidler, F., & Louis, W. (2019). Messaging matters: A systematic review of the conservation messaging literature. *Biological conservation, 236*, 92–9. https://doi.org/10.1016/j.biocon.2019.05.020

Kim, W. (2016). Economic globalization, inequality, and protest movements under capitalist political regimes, 1970–2007. *International Journal of Comparative Sociology, 57*(5), 267–287. https://doi.org/10.1177 /0020715216673414

Klandermans, B. (1984). Mobilization and participation: Social-psychological expansions of resource mobilization theory. *American Sociological Review, 49*(5), 583–600. https://doi.org/10.2307/2095417

Klandermans, B. (1997). *The Social Psychology of Protest*. Oxford: Blackwell Publishing.

Klandermans, B., De Weerd, M., Sabucedo, J. M., & Costa, M. (1999). Injustice and adversarial frames in a supranational political context: Farmers' protest in the Netherlands and Spain. In D. Della Porta & H. Kriesi (eds.), *Social Movements in a Globalizing World*. London: Palgrave Macmillan, 134–47.

Klandermans, B., van der Toorn, J., & van Stekelenburg, J. (2008). Embeddedness and identity: How immigrants turn grievances into action. *American Sociological Review, 73*(6), 992–1012. https://doi.org/10.1177 /000312240807300606

Klandermans, B., & Oegema, D. (1987). Potentials, networks, motivations and barriers: Steps towards participation in social movements. *American Sociological Review, 52*(4), 519–31. doi:https://www.jstor.org/stable/pdf/ 2095297.pdf

Klimecki, O., & Singer, T. (2012). Empathic distress fatigue rather than compassion fatigue? Integrating findings from empathy research in psychology and social neuroscience. In B. Oakley, A. Knafo, G. Madhavan, & D. S. Wilson (eds.), *Pathological Altruism*. Oxford: Oxford University Press, 368–83.

Kohn, S. (2014). Tibetan nonviolence. *Peace Review, 26*(1), 62–8. https://doi
.org/10.1080/10402659.2014.876318

Kruglanski, A. W., Bélanger, J. J., & Gunaratna, R. (2019). *The Three Pillars of
Radicalization: Needs, Narratives, and Networks*. Oxford: Oxford
University Press.

Leach, C. W., & Allen, A. M. (2017). The social psychology of the Black Lives
Matter meme and movement. *Current Directions in Psychological Science,
26*(6), 543–7. https://doi.org/10.1177/0963721417719319

Leach, C. W., Iyer, A., & Pedersen, A. (2006). Anger and guilt about ingroup
advantage explain the willingness for political action. *Personality and Social
Psychology Bulletin, 32*(9), 1232–45. https://doi.org/10.1177
/0146167206289729

Lejano, R. P., & Dodge, J. (2017). The narrative properties of ideology: The
adversarial turn and climate skepticism in the USA. *Policy Sciences, 50*(2),
195–215. https://doi.org/10.1007/s11077-016-9274-9

Lester, L., & Hutchins, B. (2009). Power games: Environmental protest, news
media and the internet. *Media, Culture and Society, 31*(4), 579–95. https://doi
.org/10.1177/0163443709335201

Lester, L., & Hutchins, B. (2012). The power of the unseen: Environmental
conflict, the media and invisibility. *Media, Culture and Society, 34*(7), 847–
63. https://doi.org/10.1177/0163443712452772

Lippmann, W. (1922). *Public Opinion*. New York: Harcourt, Brace & Co.

Livingstone, A. G. (2014). Why the psychology of collective action requires
qualitative transformation as well as quantitative change. *Contemporary
Social Science, 9*(1), 121–34. https://doi.org/10.1080/21582041
.2013.851404

Livingstone A., Spears R., Manstead A.S.R., & Bruder M. (2009). Defining
common goals without speaking the same language: Social identity and
social action in Wales. In M. Wetherell (ed.), *Theorizing Identities and
Social Action: Identity Studies in the Social Sciences*. London: Palgrave
Macmillan. https://doi.org/10.1057/9780230246942_13

Lizzio-Wilson, M., Masser, B. M., Hornsey, M. J., & Iyer, A. (2020). You're
making us all look bad: Sexism moderates women's experience of collective
threat and intra-gender hostility toward traditional and non-traditional female
subtypes. *Group Processes and Intergroup Relations*, 1368430220913610.
https://doi.org/10.1177/1368430220913610

Lizzio-Wilson, M., Thomas, E. F., Louis, W. R., Wilcockson, B., Amiot, C. E.,
Moghaddam, F. M., & McGarty, C. (2021). How collective action failure
shapes group heterogeneity and engagement in conventional and radical
action over time. *Psychological Science, 32*(4), 519–35.

Lopez, I. F. H. (2001). Protest, repression, and race: Legal violence and the Chicano movement. *University of Pennsylvania Law Review, 150*(1),205–44.

Louis, W. R. (2009). Collective action – and then what? *Journal of Social Issues, 65*(4), 727–48. https://doi.org/10.1111/j.1540-4560.2009.01623.x

Louis, W. R. , Amiot, C. E. , Thomas, E. F. , & Blackwood, L. (2016). The 'activist identity' and activism across domains: A multiple identities analysis. *Journal of Social Issues, 72*(2), 242–63.

Louis, W. R., Chonu, G. K., Achia, T., Chapman, C. M., & Rhee, J. (2018). Building group norms and identities in societal transitions from democracy to dictatorship and back again. In B. Wagoner, I. Bresco de Luna, & V. Glaveanu (eds.), *The Road To Actualized Democracy: A Psychological Exploration.* Charlotte, NC: Information Age Press, 27–57.

Louis, W. R., Duck, J. M., Terry, D. J., & Lalonde, R. N. (2010). Speaking out on immigration policy in Australia: Identity threat and the interplay of own opinion and public opinion. *Journal of Social Issues, 66*(4), 653–72. https://doi.org/10.1111/j.1540-4560.2010.01669.x

Louis, W. R., Mavor, K. I., & Terry, D. J. (2003). Reflections on the statistical analysis of personality and norms in war, peace, and prejudice: Are deviant minorities the problem? *Analyses of Social Issues and Public Policy, 3*(1), 189–98. https://doi.org/10.1111/j.1530-2415.2003.00025.x

Louis, W. R., & Montiel, C. J. (2018). Social movements and social transformation: Steps towards understanding the challenges and breakthroughs of social change. *Peace and Conflict: Journal of Peace Psychology, 24*(1), 3–9. http://dx.doi.org/10.1037/pac0000309

Louis, W. R., Taylor, D. M., & Neil, T. (2004). Cost-benefit analyses for your group and yourself: The rationality of decision-making in conflict. *International Journal of Conflict Management, 15*(2), 110–43. https://doi.org/10.1108/eb022909

Louis, W. R., Taylor, D., & Douglas, R. (2005a). Normative influence and rational conflict decisions: Group norms and cost-benefit analyses for intergroup behavior. *Group Processes and Intergroup Relations, 8*(4), 355–74. https://doi.org/10.1177/1368430205056465

Louis, W. R., Thomas, E., Chapman, C. M., Achia, T., Wibisono, S., Mirnajafi, Z., & Droogendyk, L. (2019). Emerging research on intergroup prosociality: Group members' charitable giving, positive contact, allyship, and solidarity with others. *Social and Personality Psychology Compass, 13* (3). https://doi.org/10.1111/spc3.12436

Louis, W. R., Thomas, E. F., McGarty, C., Lizzio-Wilson, M., Amiot, C., & Moghaddam, F. (2020). The volatility of collective action: Theoretical analysis and empirical data. *Advances in Political Psychology*, *41*(S1), 35–74. https://doi.org/10.1111/pops.12671

Maass, A., Clark, R. D., & Haberkorn, G. (1982). The effects of differential ascribed category membership and norms on minority influence. *European Journal of Social Psychology*, *12*(1), 89–104. https://doi.org/10.1002/ejsp.2420120107

Macy, J. (2007). *World as Self, World as Lover: Courage and Global Justice and Ecological Renewal*. Berkeley, CA: Parallax Press.

Mallett, R. K., Huntsinger, J. R., Sinclair, S., & Swim, J. K. (2008). Seeing through their eyes: When majority group members take collective action on behalf of an outgroup. *Group Processes and Intergroup Relations*, *11*(4), 451–70. https://doi.org/10.1177/1368430208095400

Margetts, H. Z., John, P., Hale, S. A., & Reissfelder, S. (2015). Leadership without leaders? Starters and followers in online collective action. *Political Studies*, *63*(2), 278–99. https://doi.org/10.1111/1467-9248.12075

Marsden, S. V. (2016). *Reintegrating Extremists: Deradicalisation and Desistance*. London: Palgrave Macmillan.

May, V. (2011). Self, belonging and social change. *Sociology*, *45*(3), 363–78.

Mazumder, S. (2018). The persistent effect of US civil rights protests on political attitudes. *American Journal of Political Science*, *62*(4), 922–35. https://doi.org/10.1111/ajps.12384

Mazzoleni, G. (2003). *The Media and the Growth of Neo-Populism in Contemporary Democracies*. London: Praeger.

McAdam, D. (1982). *Political Process and the Development of Black Insurgency, 1930–1970*. Chicago: University of Chicago Press.

McBeth, M. K., Shanahan, E. A., & Jones, M. D. (2005). The science of storytelling: Measuring policy beliefs in Greater Yellowstone. *Society and Natural Resources*, *18*(5), 413–29. https://doi.org/10.1080/08941920590924765

McCarthy, J. D., & Zald, M. N. (1977). Resource mobilization and social movements: A partial theory. *American Journal of Sociology*, *82*(6), 1212–41. https://www.jstor.org/stable/2777934

McCrae, R. R., & Costa, P. T., Jr. (1987). Validation of the five-factor model of personality across instruments and observers. *Journal of Personality and Social Psychology*, *52*(1), 81–90.

McDonald, R. I., Fielding, K. S., & Louis, W. R. (2013). Energizing and de-motivating effects of norm-conflict. *Personality and Social Psychology Bulletin*, *39*(1), 57–72. https://doi.org/10.1177/0146167212464234

McDonald, R. I., Fielding, K. S., & Louis, W. R. (2014). Conflicting norms highlight the need for action. *Environment and Behavior*, *46*(2), 139–62. https://doi.org/10.1177/0013916512453992

McGarty, C., Bliuc, A. M., Thomas, E. F., & Bongiorno, R. (2009). Collective action as the material expression of opinion-based group membership. *Journal of Social Issues*, *65*(4), 839–57. https://doi.org/10.1111/j.1540-4560.2009.01627.x

McGarty, C., Thomas, E., Blink, C., Musgrove, L., & Bliuc, A. (2006). Linking social identity, opinion, emotion, and interaction to produce long-term opinion change. *Australian Journal of Psychology*, *58*, 39.

McKimmie, B. M., Terry, D. J., Hogg, M. A., Manstead, A. S., Spears, R., & Doosje, B. (2003). I'm a hypocrite, but so is everyone else: Group support and the reduction of cognitive dissonance. *Group Dynamics: Theory, Research, and Practice*, *7*(3), 214–224. https://doi.org/10.1037/1089-2699.7.3.214

McNair, B. (2017). *An Introduction to Political Communication* (6th ed.). London: Routledge.

Metze, T., & Dodge, J. (2016). Dynamic discourse coalitions on hydro-fracking in Europe and the United States. *Environmental Communication*, *10*(3), 365–79. https://doi.org/10.1080/17524032.2015.1133437

Meyer, D. S. (2004). Protest and political opportunities. *Annual Review of Sociology*, *30*, 125–45. https://doi.org/10.1146/annurev.soc.30.012703.110545

Meyer, D. S., & Staggenborg, S. (1996). Movements, countermovements, and the structure of political opportunity. *American Journal of Sociology*, *101*(6), 1628–60. https://doi.org/10.1086/230869

Moghaddam, F. M. (2013). *The Psychology of Dictatorship*. Washington, DC: American Psychological Association.

Moghaddam, F. M. (2016). *The Psychology of Democracy*. Washington, DC: American Psychological Association.

Moghaddam, F. M. (2018). *Mutual radicalization: How Groups and Nations Drive Each Other to Extremes*. Washington, DC: American Psychological Association.

Monaghan, J., & Walby, K. (2012). 'They attacked the city': Security intelligence, the sociology of protest policing and the anarchist threat at the 2010 Toronto G20 summit. *Current Sociology*, *60*(5), 653–71. https://doi.org/10.1177/0011392112448470

Mooijman, M., Hoover, J., Lin, Y., Ji, H., & Dehghani, M. (2018). Moralization in social networks and the emergence of violence during protests. *Nature Human Behaviour*, *2*(6), 389–96. https://doi.org/10.1038/s41562-018-0353-0

Moscovici, S., Lage, E., & Naffrechoux, M. (1969). Influence of a consistent minority on the responses of a majority in a color perception task. *Sociometry*, *32*(4), 365–80. https://doi.org/10.2307/2786541

Moskalenko, S., & McCauley, C. (2009). Measuring political mobilization: The distinction between activism and radicalism. *Terrorism and Political Violence, 21*(2), 239–60. https://doi.org/10.1080/09546550902765508

Moskalenko, S., & McCauley, C. (2011). The psychology of lone-wolf terrorism. *Counselling Psychology Quarterly, 24*(2), 115–26. https://doi.org /10.1080/09515070.2011.581835

Mudde, C. (2007). Radical right parties in Europe: What, who, why? *Participation, 34*(3), 12–15.

Muis, J., & Immerzeel, T. (2017). Causes and consequences of the rise of populist radical right parties and movements in Europe. *Current Sociology, 65*(6), 909–30. https://doi.org/10.1177/0011392117717294

Mundt, M., Ross, K., & Burnett, C. M. (2018). Scaling social movements through social media: The case of Black Lives Matter. *Social Media and Society, 4*(4), 2056305118807911. https://doi.org/10.1177 /2056305118807911

Munro, E. (2013). Feminism: A fourth wave? *Political Insight, 4*(2), 22–5.

Nagle, A. (2017). *Kill all Normies: The Online Culture Wars from Tumblr and 4chan to the Alt-Right and Trump.* Winchester: Zero Books.

Nisbet, M. C. (2009). Communicating climate change: Why frames matter for public engagement. *Environment: Science and Policy for Sustainable Development, 51*(2), 12–23.

Newman, T. P., Nisbet, E. C., & Nisbet, M. C. (2018). Climate change, cultural cognition, and media effects: Worldviews drive news selectivity, biased processing, and polarized attitudes. *Public Understanding of Science, 27* (8), 985–1002.

Norton, T. , & Grecu, N. (2015). Publics, communication campaigns, and persuasive communication. In A. Hansen & R. Cox (eds.), *The Routledge Handbook of Environment and Communication.* London: Routledge, 374–87.

Ntontis, E., & Hopkins, N. (2018). Framing a 'social problem': Emotion in anti-abortion activists' depiction of the abortion debate. *British Journal of Social Psychology, 57*(3), 666–83. https://doi.org/10.1111/bjso.12249

Oegema, D., & Klandermans, B. (1994). Why social movement sympathizers don't participate: Erosion and nonconversion of support. *American Sociological Review, 59*(5), 703–22. https://doi.org/10.2307/2096444

Orazani, S. N., & Leidner, B. (2019). A case for social change in Iran: Greater support and mobilization potential for nonviolent than violent social movements. *Peace and Conflict: Journal of Peace Psychology, 25*(1), 3–12. https://doi.org/10.1037/pac0000349

Osborne, D., Jost, J. T., Becker, J. C., Badaan, V., & Sibley, C. G. (2018). Protesting to challenge or defend the system? A system justification perspective on collective action. *European Journal of Social Psychology, 49*, 244–69. https://doi.org/10.1002/ejsp.2522

Packer, D. J. (2009). Avoiding groupthink: Whereas weakly identified members remain silent, strongly identified members dissent about collective problems. *Psychological Science, 20*(5), 546–48.

Pareto, V. (1935). *The Mind and Society.* New York: Dover.

Parker, K., Horowitz, J. M., & Anderson, M. (2020). Amid protests, majorities across racial and ethnic groups express support for the Black Lives Matter Movement. Retrieved from: www.pewsocialtrends.org/2020/06/12/amid-protests-majorities-across-racial-and-ethnic-groups-express-support-for-the-black-lives-matter-movement.

Paxton, P., Hughes, M. M., & Green, J. L. (2006). The international women's movement and women's political representation, 1893–2003. *American Sociological Review, 71*(6), 898–920. https://doi.org/10.1177/000312240607100602

Platow, M. J., Eggins, R. A., Chattopadhyay, R., Brewer, G., Hardwick, L., Milsom, L., Brocklebank, J., Lalor, T., Martin, R., Quee, M. & Vassallo, S. (2013). Two experimental tests of relational models of procedural justice: Non-instrumental voice and authority group membership. *British Journal of Social Psychology, 52*(2), 361–76.

Pratt, D. (2015). Islamophobia as reactive co-radicalization. *Islam and Christian–Muslim Relations, 26*(2), 205–18. https://doi.org/10.1080/09596410.2014.1000025

Ray, R. (2020). Setting the record straight on the Movement for Black Lives. *Ethnic and Racial Studies, 43*(8), 1393–1401. https://doi.org/10.1080/01419870.2020.1718727

Rees, J. H., & Bamberg, S. (2014). Climate protection needs societal change: Determinants of intention to participate in collective climate action. *European Journal of Social Psychology, 44*(5), 466–73.

Reicher, S., Cassidy, C., Wolpert, I., Hopkins, N., & Levine, M. (2006). Saving Bulgaria's Jews: An analysis of social identity and the mobilisation of social solidarity. *European Journal of Social Psychology, 36*(1), 49–72. https://doi.org/10.1002/ejsp.291

Reicher, S., Hopkins, N., Levine, M., & Rath, R. (2005). Entrepreneurs of hate and entrepreneurs of solidarity: Social identity as a basis for mass communication. *International Review of the Red Cross, 87*(860), 621–37. https://doi.org/10.1017/S1816383100184462

Reimer, N. K., Becker, J. C., Benz, A., Christ, O., Dhont, K., Klocke, U., Hewstone, M. (2017). Intergroup contact and social change: Implications of negative and positive contact for collective action in advantaged and disadvantaged groups. *Personality and Social Psychology Bulletin, 43*(1), 121–36. https://doi.org/10.1177/0146167216676478

Richter, L., Cordner, A., & Brown, P. (2018). Non-stick science: Sixty years of research and (in)action on fluorinated compounds. *Social Studies of Science, 48*(5), 691–714. https://doi.org/10.1177/0306312718799960

Robbins, T. (1984). Constructing cultist 'mind control'. *Sociological Analysis, 45*(3), 241–56. https://www.jstor.org/stable/3711480

Rooduijn, M. (2015). The rise of the populist radical right in Western Europe. *European View, 14*(1), 3–11. https://doi.org/10.1007/s12290-015-0347-5

Runciman, W. (1966). *Relative Deprivation and Social Justice: A Study of Attitudes to Social Inequality in Twentieth-Century England.* Berkeley, CA: University of California Press.

Saab, R., Tausch, N., Spears, R., & Cheung, W. Y. (2015). Acting in solidarity: Testing an extended dual pathway model of collective action by bystander group members. *British Journal of Social Psychology, 54*(3), 539–60. https://doi.org/10.1111/bjso.12095

Sabatier, P. A. (1998). The advocacy coalition framework: Revisions and relevance for Europe. *Journal of European Public Policy, 5*(1), 98–130. https://doi.org/10.1080/13501768880000051

Sabatier, P. A., & Jenkins-Smith, H. C. (1993). The advocacy coalition framework: Assessment, revisions, and implications for scholars and practitioners. In *Policy Change and Learning: An Advocacy Coalition Approach.* Boulder, CO: Westview Press, 211–36.

Sani, F., & Reicher, S. (1998). When consensus fails: An analysis of the schism within the Italian Communist Party (1991). *European Journal of Social Psychology, 28*(4), 623–45.

Sani, F., & Reicher, S. (2000). Contested identities and schisms in groups: Opposing the ordination of women as priests in the Church of England. *British Journal of Social Psychology, 39*(1), 95–112. https://doi.org/10.1348/014466600164354

Schulte, M., Bamberg, S., Rees, J., & Rollin, P. (2020). Social identity as a key concept for connecting transformative societal change with individual environmental activism. *Journal of Environmental Psychology, 72,* 101525.

Schultz, P. W., Nolan, J. M., Cialdini, R. B., Goldstein, N. J., & Griskevicius, V. (2007). The constructive, destructive, and reconstructive power of social norms. *Psychological Science, 18*(5), 429–34. https://doi.org/10.1111/j.1467-9280.2007.01917.x

Sharp, G. (1973). *The Politics of Nonviolent Action* (vol. 1). Boston: Sargent Publisher.

Siegel, D. A. (2011). When does repression work? Collective action in social networks. *The Journal of Politics*, *73*(4), 993–1010.

Simcox, R., Stuart, H., & Ahmed, H. (2010). *Islamist Terrorism: The British Connections*. London: The Henry Jackson Society.

Simon, B., & Grabow, O. (2010). The Politicization of migrants: Further evidence that politicized collective identity is a dual identity. *Political Psychology*, *31*(5), 717–38. https://doi.org/10.1111/j.1467-9221.2010.00782.x

Simon, B., & Klandermans, B. (2001). Politicized collective identity: A social psychological analysis. *American Psychologist*, *56*(4), 319–31. https://doi.org/10.1037//0003-066x.56.4.319

Simpson, B., Willer, R., & Feinberg, M. (2018). Does violent protest backfire? Testing a theory of public reactions to activist violence. *Socius: Sociological Research for a Dynamic World*, *4*, 1–14. https://doi.org/10.1177/2378023118803189

Small, D. A., Loewenstein, G., & Slovic, P. (2007). Sympathy and callousness: The impact of deliberative thought on donations to identifiable and statistical victims. *Organizational Behavior and Human Decision Processes*, *102*, 143–53. https://doi.org/10.1016/j.obhdp.2006.01.005

Smith, J., Louis, W. R., Terry, D. J., Greenaway, K. H., Clarke, M. R., & Cheng, X. (2012). Congruent or conflicted? The impact of injunctive and descriptive norms on environmental intentions. *Journal of Environmental Psychology*, *32*(4), 353–61. https://doi.org/10.1016/j.jenvp.2012.06.001

Smith, J. R., & Louis, W. R. (2008). Do as we say and as we do: The interplay of descriptive and injunctive group norms in the attitude–behavior relationship. *British Journal of Social Psychology*, *47*, 647–66. https://doi.org/10.1348/014466607X269748

Smith, J. R., & Louis, W. R. (2009). Group norms and the attitude–behaviour relationship. *Social and Personality Psychology Compass*, *3*(1), 19–35. https://doi.org/10.1111/j.1751-9004.2008.00161.x

Smith, L. G., Blackwood, L., & Thomas, E. F. (2020). The need to refocus on the group as the site of radicalization. *Perspectives on Psychological Science*, *15*(2), 327–52. https://doi.org/10.1177/1745691619885870

Smith, L. G., Livingstone, A. G., & Thomas, E. F. (2019). Advancing the social psychology of rapid societal change. *British Journal of Social Psychology*, *58*(1), 33–44. https://doi.org/10.1111/bjso.12292

Smith, L. G., Thomas, E. F., & McGarty, C. (2015). 'We must be the change we want to see in the world': Integrating norms and identities through social interaction. *Political Psychology*, *36*(5), 543–57. https://doi.org/10.1111/pops.12180

Snow, D. A., & Benford, R. D. (1988). Ideology, frame resonance, and participant mobilization. In B. Klandersman, H. Kriesi, & S. G. Tarrow (eds.), *From Structure to Action: Comparing Social Movement Research across Cultures*. Greenwich: JAI Press.

Soares, M., Barbosa, M., & Matos, R. (2018). Police officers' perspectives on state (police) violence: A sociomoral and psychological-driven study on disengagement. *Journal of Social and Political Psychology*, *6*(1), 174–204. https://doi.org/10.5964/jspp.v6i1.597

Sotirov, M., & Winkel, G. (2016). Toward a cognitive theory of shifting coalitions and policy change: Linking the advocacy coalition framework and cultural theory. *Policy Sciences*, *49*(2), 125–54. https://doi.org/10.1007/s11077-015-9235-8

Spears, R. (2010). Group rationale, collective sense: Beyond intergroup bias. *British Journal of Social Psychology*, *49*(1), 1–20. https://doi.org/10.1348/014466609X481308

Staggenborg, S. (1998). Social movement communities and cycles of protest: The emergence and maintenance of a local women's movement. *Social Problems*, *45*(2), 180–204. https://doi.org/10.2307/3097243

Steffens, N. K., Haslam, S. A., Ryan, M. K., & Kessler, T. (2013). Leader performance and prototypicality: Their inter-relationship and impact on leaders' identity entrepreneurship. *European Journal of Social Psychology*, *43*(7), 606–13. https://doi.org/10.1002/ejsp.1985

Stephan, M. J., & Chenoweth, E. (2008). Why civil resistance works: The strategic logic of nonviolent conflict. *International security*, *33*(1), 7–44.

Stock, P. V. (2014). The perennial nature of the Catholic Worker farms: A reconsideration of failure. *Rural Sociology*, *79*(2), 143–73. https://doi.org/10.1111/ruso.12029

Stott, C., Livingstone, A., & Hoggett, J. (2008). Policing football crowds in England and Wales: a model of 'good practice'?. *Policing and Society*, *18*(3), 258–81. https://doi.org/10.1080/10439460802091641

Stott, C., & Reicher, S. (2011). *Mad Mobs and Englishmen? Myths and Realities of the 2011 Riots*. London: Constable & Robinson.

Stuart, A., Thomas, E. F., & Donaghue, N. (2018). 'I don't really want to be associated with the self-righteous left extreme': Disincentives to participation in collective action. *Journal of Social and Political Psychology*, *6*(1), 242–70. https://doi.org/10.5964/jspp.v6i1.567

Stuart, A., Thomas, E. F., Donaghue, N., & Russell, A. (2013). 'We may be pirates, but we are not protesters': Identity in the Sea Shepherd Conservation Society. *Political Psychology*, *34*(5), 753–77. https://doi.org/10.1111/pops.12016

Subasic, E., Reynolds, K. J., & Turner, J. C. (2008). The political solidarity model of social change: Dynamics of self-categorization in intergroup power relations. *Personality and Social Psychology Review, 12*(4), 330–52. https://doi.org/10.1177/1088868308323223

Subasic, E., Schmitt, M. T., & Reynolds, K. J. (2011). Are we all in this together? Co-victimization, inclusive social identity and collective action in solidarity with the disadvantaged. *British Journal of Social Psychology, 50* (4), 707–25. https://doi.org/10.1111/j.2044-8309.2011.02073.x

Thomas, E. F., Zubielevitch, E., Sibley, C. G., & Osborne, D. (2020). Testing the social identity model of collective action longitudinally and across structurally disadvantaged and advantaged groups. *Personality and Social Psychology Bulletin, 46*(6), 823–38.

Sweetman, J., Leach, C. W., Spears, R., Pratto, F., & Saab, R. (2013). 'I have a dream': A typology of social change goals. *Journal of Social and Political Psychology, 1*(1), 293–320.

Tajfel, H., & Turner, J. C. (1979). An integrative theory of inter-group conflict. In W. G. Austin & S. Worchel (eds.), *The Social Psychology of Intergroup Relations*. Monterey, CA: Brooks-Cole, 33–47.

Tarrow, S., & Tilly, C. (2007). Contentious politics and social movements. In C. Boix & S. C. Stokes (eds.), *The Oxford Handbook of Comparative Politics*. Oxford: Oxford University Press. https://doi.org/10.1093/oxfordhb/9780199566020.003.0019

Tarrow, S. G. (2011). *Power in Movement: Social Movements and Contentious Politics*. Cambridge: Cambridge University Press.

Tausch, N., Becker, J. C., Spears, R., Christ, O., Saab, R., Singh, P., & Siddiqui, R. N. (2011). Explaining radical group behavior: Developing emotion and efficacy routes to normative and nonnormative collective action. *Journal of Personality and Social Psychology, 101*(1), 129–48. https://doi.org/10.1037/a0022728

Tausch, N., Saguy, T., & Bryson, J. (2015). How does intergroup contact affect social change? Its impact on collective action and individual mobility intentions among members of a disadvantaged group. *Journal of Social Issues, 71* (3), 536–53. https://doi.org/10.1111/josi.12127

Teixeira, C. P., Spears, R., & Yzerbyt, V. Y. (2019). Is Martin Luther King or Malcom X the more acceptable face of protest? High-status groups' reactions to low-status groups' collective action. *Journal of Personality and Social Psychology, 118*(5):919–44. https://doi.org/10.1037/pspi0000195

Terry, D. J., Hogg, M. A., & White, K. M. (1999). The theory of planned behaviour: Self-identity, social identity and group norms. *British Journal of Social Psychology, 38*, 225–44. https://doi.org/10.1348/014466699164149

Thomas, E. F., Bury, S. M., Louis, W. R., Amiot, C. E., Molenberghs, P., Crane, M. F., & Decety, J. (2019). Vegetarian, vegan, activist, radical: Using latent profile analysis to examine different forms of support for animal welfare. *Group Processes and Intergroup Relations*, *22*(6), 836–57. https://doi.org/10.1177/1368430218824407

Thomas, E. F., & Louis, W. R. (2013). Doing democracy: The social psychological mobilization and consequences of collective action. *Social Issues and Policy Review*, *7*(1), 173–200. https://doi.org/10.1111/j.1751-2409.2012.01047.x

Thomas, E. F., Mavor, K. I., & McGarty, C. (2012). Social identities facilitate and encapsulate action-relevant constructs: A test of the social identity model of collective action. *Group Processes and Intergroup Relations*, *15*(1), 75–88. https://doi.org/10.1177/1368430211413619

Thomas, E. F., McGarty, C., & Louis, W. (2014). Social interaction and psychological pathways to political engagement and extremism. *European Journal of Social Psychology*, *44*(1), 15–22. https://doi.org/10.1002/ejsp.1988

Thomas, E. F., & McGarty, C. (2018). Giving versus acting: Using latent profile analysis to distinguish between benevolent and activist support for global poverty reduction. *British Journal of Social Psychology*, *57*(1), 189–209. https://doi.org/10.1111/bjso.12228

Thomas, E. F., McGarty, C., Lala, G., Stuart, A., Hall, L. J., & Goddard, A. (2015). Whatever happened to Kony2012? Understanding a global Internet phenomenon as an emergent social identity. *European Journal of Social Psychology*, *45*(3), 356–67. https://doi.org/10.1002/ejsp.2094

Thomas, E. F., McGarty, C., & Louis, W. R. (2014). Social interaction and psychological pathways to political engagement and extremism. *European Journal of Social Psychology*, *44*(1), 15–22. https://doi.org/10.1002/ejsp.1988

Thomas, E. F., McGarty, C., & Mavor, K. I. (2009). Aligning identities, emotions, and beliefs to create commitment to sustainable social and political action. *Personality and Social Psychology Review*, *13*(3), 194–218. https://doi.org/10.1177/1088868309341563

Thomas, E. F., McGarty, C., Reese, G., Berndsen, M., & Bliuc, A.-M. (2016). Where there is a (collective) will, there are (effective) ways: Integrating individual- and group-level factors in explaining humanitarian collective action. *Personality and Social Psychology Bulletin*, *42*(12), 1678–92. https://doi.org/10.1177/0146167216669134

Thomas, E. F., McGarty, C., Stuart, A., Smith, L. G., & Bourgeois, L. (2019). Reaching consensus promotes the internalization of commitment to social change. *Group Processes & Intergroup Relations*, *22*(5), 615–30. https://doi .org/10.1177/1368430218780320

Thomas, E. F., Rathmann, L., & McGarty, C. (2017). From 'I' to 'we': Different forms of identity, emotion, and belief predict victim support volunteerism among nominal and active supporters. *Journal of Applied Social Psychology*, *47*(4), 213–23. https://doi.org/10.1111/jasp.12428

Tilly, C. (1999). From interactions to outcomes in social movements. In M. Giugni, D. McAdam, C. Tilly, & S. Tarrow (eds.), *How Social Movements Matter*. Minneapolis, MN: University of Minnesota Press, 253–70. https://www.jstor.org/stable/10.5749/j.ctttt706

Turner, J. C., Hogg, M. A., Oakes, P. J., Reicher, S. D., & Wetherell, M. S. (1987). *Rediscovering the Social Group: A Self-Categorization Theory*. Oxford: Basil Blackwell.

Uluğ, Ö. M., & Acar, Y. G. (2018). What happens after the protests? Understanding protest outcomes through multi-level social change. *Peace and Conflict: Journal of Peace Psychology*, *24*(1), 44–53. https://doi.org/10 .1037/pac0000269

Unsworth, K. L., & Fielding, K. S. (2014). It's political: How the salience of one's political identity changes climate change beliefs and policy support. *Global Environmental Change*, *27*, 131–7. https://doi.org/10.1016/j .gloenvcha.2014.05.002

van Dyke, N., & Amos, B. (2017). Social movement coalitions: Formation, longevity, and success. *Sociology Compass*, *11*(7), e12489. https://doi.org/10 .1111/soc4.12489

van Zomeren, M. (2013). Four core social-psychological motivations to under-take collective action. *Social and Personality Psychology Compass*, *7*(6), 378–88. https://doi.org/10.1111/spc3.12031

van Zomeren, M., & Iyer, A. (2009). Introduction to the social and psycho-logical dynamics of collective action. *Journal of Social Issues*, *65*(4), 645–60. https://doi.org/10.1111/j.1540-4560.2009.01618.x

van Zomeren, M., & Louis, W. R. (2017). Culture meets collective action: Exciting synergies and some lessons to learn for the future. *Group Processes and Intergroup Relations*, *20*(3), 277–84. https://doi.org/10.1177 /1368430217690238

van Zomeren, M., Postmes, T., & Spears, R. (2008). Toward an integrative social identity model of collective action: A quantitative research synthesis of three socio-psychological perspectives. *Psychological Bulletin*, *134*(4), 504–35. https://doi.org/10.1037/0033-2909.134.4.504

van Zomeren, M., Postmes, T., & Spears, R. (2012). On conviction's collective consequences: Integrating moral conviction with the social identity model of collective action. *British Journal of Social Psychology, 51*(1), 52–71. https://doi.org/10.1111/j.2044-8309.2010.02000.x

van Zomeren, M. , Spears, R. , Fischer, A. H. , & Leach, C. W. (2004). Put your money where your mouth is! Explaining collective action tendencies through group-based anger and group efficacy. *Journal of Personality and Social Psychology, 87*(5), 649–64.

Vehlken, S. (2013). Zootechnologies: Swarming as a cultural technique. *Theory, Culture and Society, 30*(6), 110–31.

Vestergren, S., Drury, J., & Chiriac, E. H. (2018). How collective action produces psychological change and how that change endures over time: A case study of an environmental campaign. *British Journal of Social Psychology, 57*(4), 855–77. https://doi.org/10.1111/bjso.12270

Wagoner, B., Moghaddam, F. M., & Valsiner, J. (2018). *The Psychology of Radical Social Change: From Rage to Revolution.* Cambridge: Cambridge University Press.

Wasow, O. (2020). Agenda seeding: How 1960s Black protests moved elites, public opinion and voting. *American Political Science Review, 114*(3), 1–22. https://doi.org/10.1017/S000305542000009X

Weaver, D. H. (2007). Thoughts on agenda setting, framing, and priming. *Journal of Communication, 57*(1), 142–7. https://doi.org/10.1111/j.1460-2466.2006.00333.x

Webb, T. L., & Sheeran, P. (2006). Does changing behavioral intentions engender behavior change? A meta-analysis of the experimental evidence. *Psychological Bulletin, 132*(2), 249–68. https://doi.org/10.1037/0033-2909.132.2.249

Webber, D., Babush, M., Schori-Eyal, N., Vazeou-Nieuwenhuis, A., Hettiarachchi, M., Belanger, J. J., & Gelfand, M. J. (2017). The road to extremism: Field and experimental evidence that significance loss-induced need for closure fosters radicalization. *Journal of Personality and Social Psychology, 114*(2), 270–85. https://doi.org/10.1037/pspi0000111

Webber, D., & Kruglanski, A. W. (2018). The social psychological makings of a terrorist. *Current Opinion in Psychology, 19*, 131–4. https://doi.org/10.1016/j.copsyc.2017.03.024

Weible, C. M., & Sabatier, P. A. (2007). A guide to the advocacy coalition framework. In F. Fischer & G. J. Miller (eds.), *Handbook of Public Policy Analysis: Theory, Politics, and Methods.* Milton Park: Taylor & Francis Group, 123–36.

Whitehouse, H., Jong, J., Buhrmester, M. D., Gómez, Á., Bastian, B., Kavanagh, C. M., & McKay, R. (2017). The evolution of extreme cooperation via shared dysphoric experiences. *Scientific Reports, 7*, 44292. https://doi.org/10.1038/srep44292

Whitehouse, H., McQuinn, B., Buhrmester, M., & Swann, W. B. (2014). Brothers in arms: Libyan revolutionaries bond like family. *Proceedings of the National Academy of Sciences, 111*(50), 17783–5.

Williamson, V., Trump, K. S., & Einstein, K. L. (2018). Black Lives Matter: Evidence that police-caused deaths predict protest activity. *Perspectives on Politics, 16*(2), 400–15. https://doi.org/10.1017/S1537592717004273

Wright, S. C., & Taylor, D. M. (1998). Responding to tokenism: Individual action in the face of collective injustice. *European Journal of Social Psychology, 28*(4), 647–67.

Wright, S. C., Taylor, D. M., & Moghaddam, F. M. (1990). Responding to membership in a disadvantaged group – from acceptance to collective protest. *Journal of Personality and Social Psychology, 58*(6), 994–1003. https://doi.org/10.1037/0022-3514.58.6.994

Zaal, M. P., Laar, C. V., Ståhl, T., Ellemers, N., & Derks, B. (2011). By any means necessary: The effects of regulatory focus and moral conviction on hostile and benevolent forms of collective action. *British Journal of Social Psychology, 50*(4), 670–89. https://doi.org/10.1111/j.2044-8309.2011.02069.x

Zak, P. J., & Barraza, J. A. (2013). The neurobiology of collective action. *Frontiers in Neuroscience, 7,* 211. https://doi.org/10.3389/fnins.2013.00211

Cambridge Elements ≡

Applied Social Psychology

Susan Clayton
College of Wooster, Ohio
Susan Clayton is a social psychologist at the College of Wooster in Wooster, Ohio. Her research focuses on the human relationship with nature, how it is socially constructed, and how it can be utilised to promote environmental concern.

About the Series
Many social psychologists have used their research to understand and address pressing social issues, from poverty and prejudice to work and health. Each Element in this series reviews a particular area of applied social psychology. Elements will also discuss applications of the research findings and describe directions for future study.

Applied Social Psychology

Elements in the Series

Printed in the United States
by Baker & Taylor Publisher Services